Artist: Francine Auger

Nellie McClung, 1873-1951.

*Nellie L. McClung*

# Margaret Macpherson

Margaret Macpherson is a creative nonfiction writer living in Edmonton. She has published four books, most of them based on the history of northwestern Canada and the western United States. *Silk, Spices and Glory: In Search of the Northwest Passage*, published by Fifth House, a division of Fitzhenry & Whiteside, was cited in the press as "history infused with soul and immediacy."

Macpherson has worked as a journalist and essayist for over twenty years. Her work has won prizes in *Grain* magazine's Long Grain of Truth competition, 2000 and the Banff Centre for the Arts Jon Whyte Memorial Essay Competition, 1999 and 2002. These prize-winning creative nonfiction essays and short stories have been published in select literary magazines across Canada. Macpherson is a former associate editor for *NeWest Review*, Saskatoon; *Other Voices*, Edmonton; and *Prism International*, Vancouver. She regularly publishes literary reviews in the *Edmonton Journal*. Macpherson holds a Master of Fine Arts degree in Creative Writing from the University of British Columbia and, like Nellie McClung, is a member of the Canadian Authors Association.

## In the same collection

Ven Begamudré, *Isaac Brock: Larger Than Life*.

Lynne Bowen, *Robert Dunsmuir: Laird of the Mines*.

Kate Braid, *Emily Carr: Rebel Artist*.

Kathryn Bridge, *Phyllis Munday: Mountaineer*.

William Chalmers, *George Mercer Dawson: Geologist, Scientist, Explorer*.

Judith Fitzgerald, *Marshall McLuhan: Wise Guy*.

lian goodall, *William Lyon Mackenzie King: Dreams and Shadows*.

Stephen Eaton Hume, *Frederick Banting: Hero, Healer, Artist*.

Naïm Kattan, *A.M. Klein: Poet and Prophet*.

Betty Keller, *Pauline Johnson: First Aboriginal Voice of Canada*.

Michelle Labrèche-Larouche, *Emma Albani: International Star*.

Dave Margoshes, *Tommy Douglas: Building the New Society*.

Raymond Plante, *Jacques Plante: Behind the Mask*.

T.F. Rigelhof, *George Grant: Redefining Canada*.

Arthur Slade, *John Diefenbaker: An Appointment with Destiny*.

Roderick Stewart, *Wilfrid Laurier: A Pledge for Canada*.

John Wilson, *John Franklin: Traveller on Undiscovered Seas*.

John Wilson, *Norman Bethune: A Life of Passionate Conviction*.

Rachel Wyatt, *Agnes Macphail: Champion of the Underdog*.

# Nellie McClung

**National Library of Canada cataloguing in publication**

Macpherson, M. A. (Margaret A.), 1959-

    Nellie McClung: voice for the voiceless

    (The Quest library ; 20).
    Includes bibliographical references and index.

    ISBN 1-894852-04-4

    1. McClung, Nellie L., 1873-1951. 2. Feminists – Canada – Biography. 3. Authors, Canadian (English) – 20th century – Biography. I. Title. II. Series: Quest library; 20.

HQ1455.M3M32 2003      305.42'092      C2003-940866-3

Legal Deposit: Second quarter 2003
National Library of Canada
Bibliothèque nationale du Québec

XYZ Publishing acknowledges the support of The Quest Library project by the Canadian Studies Program and the Book Publishing Industry Development Program (BPIDP) of the Department of Canadian Heritage. The opinions expressed do not necessarily reflect the views of the Government of Canada.

The publishers further acknowledge the financial support our publishing program receives from The Canada Council for the Arts, the ministère de la Culture et des Communications du Québec, and the Société de développement des entreprises culturelles.

Chronology: Lynne Bowen
Index: Darcy Dunton
Layout: Édiscript enr.
Cover design: Zirval Design
Cover illustration: Francine Auger
Photo research: Margaret Macpherson and Rhonda Bailey
Editorial Assistant: Nigel Cass

Printed and bound in Canada

XYZ Publishing
1781 Saint Hubert Street
Montreal, Quebec  H2L 3Z1
Tel: (514) 525-2170
Fax: (514) 525-7537
E-mail: info@xyzedit.qc.ca
Web site: www.xyzedit.qc.ca

Distributed by: Fitzhenry & Whiteside
195 Allstate Parkway
Markham, ON L3R 4T8
Customer Service, tel: (905) 477-9700
Toll free ordering, tel: 1-800-387-9776
Fax: 1-800-260-9777
E-mail: bookinfo@fitzhenry.ca

MARGARET MACPHERSON

# Nellie McCLUNG

VOICE FOR THE VOICELESS

Publishing

*Remembering my mother,*
*Ethel Fairbank Macpherson*
*– tough, tender, and true.*

# Contents

Women's work was endless and repetitive in early settler society.
None of it appeals to young Nellie Letitia Mooney.

The annual pig kill strikes horror into the heart of a young Nellie,
but it is an essential part of life on the Mooney homestead.

# 1

## *The Golden Promise*

*"I have always regarded the fact that I was born and brought up in the country as one of the happiest circumstances of my life... Country people have time to tidy up their minds, classify their emotions, and, generally, get their souls into shape."*
*– NLM*

"It's not fair."

Stomping her foot on the bleached pine floor of the farmhouse, five-year-old Nellie Letitia Mooney wailed loud and long. "Not fair." Stomp. Stomp. "Not fair. Not fair."

The window was streaked with rain, but she could still see brother Jack clamber into the wagon beside their father. The pony surged forward and the two headed down Garafraxa Road to town. Tears of anger and resentment sprang to Nellie's eyes. "Why can Jack go, if I can't? And what about Hannah? Why do we always have to stay home? It's not fair."

She buried her face in the rough, spun wool curtains, which, not so long ago, had been one of Lizzie's dresses and still bore her sweet smell. As though to add insult to injury, the rod clattered down and the fabric puddled at Nellie's feet. Outside the bare window, there wasn't even a puff of dust, the conspiring rain had seen to that. The wagon, with chosen Jack, had disappeared.

Nellie kicked at the fallen window cover and tried to connect foot to floor in one final stomp, but Letitia, her mother, sprang forward to yank her youngest out of the tangled mess.

"Enough dramatics, Nellie," said the stern, stout woman, brushing both child and cloth off with a practised hand. The light from the now bare window caught her attention and she looked out. "It's clearing," she muttered, and then spoke to the child, "The moon is right tonight and we've soap to make. The men have gone to Chatsworth to get supplies for tomorrow's kill. Now, off you go with Hannah and stoke the fire in the back yard. And don't forget the leach."

*The pig kill! Soap-making! Stoke the fire! Water the leach! It's always the same. Boys get the adventure and girls get the work.* Nellie fumed.

The huge black cauldron used exclusively for making soap was steaming and smoking in the backyard. The early morning drizzle had stopped, and a weak, watery sun dissolved most of the grey clouds. The family dogs, Nap and Watch, idled around the fire, curious about the activity, and Nellie's older sister Hannah, who seemed not at all perturbed by Jack's preferential treatment, was already poking dry sticks into the hissing embers.

Nellie's mood matched the steaming water. Still, she knew what had to be done if soap was to set by evening. The barrel of ashes perched on its trestle, and Nellie's job was to keep water constantly flowing through the ash. When the leach was running, her mother gathered the black lye that seeped out the bottom of the barrel. This slimy mixture was boiled with grease in the black kettle until the gooey lye and slick grease fused. Nellie tended the leach, Hannah looked after the fire, Lizzie managed the wooden soapboxes on the windward side of the kettle, and their mother did the serious work of stirring the boiling mixture until that exact moment when the soap was ready.

And where was Jack when all this hard work was going on? Why, Jack was likely in town right now, all puffed up with manly pride, buying penny candy. He was only ten years old, only five years older than Nellie, not a man at all.

Water sluiced over the barrel lip and some of the ash spilled out the top of the wooden leach. Nellie had poured too fast. It was all Jack's fault. Life was not fair.

∽

Nellie Letitia Mooney was born on October 20, 1873 in Grey County, Ontario, the sixth and last child of Letitia and John Mooney. The homestead was well established by the time Nellie came along, but despite fifteen years of labour, it was a patch of ground that still produced more rocks than feed. John Mooney, an Irishman, was resigned to his lot in life, but his wife was not. She was twenty years younger and still optimistic.

John was a recently widowed shantyman when Letitia, a Scottish immigrant, met him in Bytown, Ontario. His first wife, a cousin, had lived only a year after John acquired the sixty stony hectares on the Garafraxa Road. Unlike Letitia, the first wife was spared the poverty of her land, but her grave revealed the thin topsoil and the multitude of stones. Letitia recognized at once that this land was best suited for graves not grain. Still, after her wedding, she moved into the whitewashed farmhouse one and a half kilometres south of Chatsworth, planted a few fruit trees, and dug in to survive. The year was 1858. The children came quickly, and through it all – the rock picking and plowing, lean times and harsh winters – John never lost the lilt in his voice or the easy smile that betrayed his Irish roots.

William, the eldest Mooney, was almost fifteen years Nellie's senior, but he was her champion and devoted friend. George, two years younger then William, was a boy with bulging pockets and an impish grin; he was always on the hunt for a good trade. Elizabeth came next; she was a lovely girl with a buttermilk complexion and the ability to understand how very difficult it was to keep dresses clean. Hannah, Nellie's closest sister, was three years her senior and a startling contrast to the spirited chatterbox who completed the family. Hannah spoke only when spoken to.

She was serious and introspective, the polar opposite of her little sister. Jack was five years older then Nellie. While Nellie may have been the precious youngest child, Jack would always be the precious youngest son.

∞

Soap-making was one of many chores typical of the Ontario pioneer farm wife in the latter half of the 1800s. The entire Mooney family, men and women together, planted and harvested in the spring and autumn, and while the men worked the land and took care of the livestock, Letitia and her three daughters made candles, churned butter and cheese, and baked bread. Theirs too were the seasonal tasks of weeding the garden, pruning the fruit trees, drying dandelion roots for coffee, and preserving fruit, pickles, and berries. They took care of the family clothing – spinning and dyeing wool, knitting or sewing new garments, and making over old clothing for other uses. They also washed clothes. There was always a great amount of laundry to do and it was a day-long task involving a huge fire, scalded hands, and the acrid smell of soap and sweat. Looking after the poultry was also women's work, as was smoking hams and salting pork in preparation for winter.

∞

Nellie knew the pig kill was coming, and all day her dread mounted. Cakes of soap had cooled into creamy perfection the night before, and Letitia was satisfied with the day's work. She'd come to Nellie and Hannah's room to talk about the dreaded chore ahead. "You're so like your father, Nellie. You know, when he was a boy he used to run to the bog when the pigs were killed. But as a man, he's learned to do it himself, so it can be done quickly with little suffering."

That morning, Nellie felt the farm was alive with fear. There was a sickness in the pit of her belly and panic shot through the air. Even the dark clouds mirrored Nellie's foreboding. They cast an odd green gloom over the proceeding. As the pigs squealed and snorted with raw nervous energy and the gruesome scaffold was erected by her father and brothers, Nellie grew more and more agitated. "I feel as though my heart will break," she cried, clutching Lizzie's hand. "The poor pigs. Do they know today is the day they'll die?"

"Hush, Nellie. We'll go to the lower meadow," whispered her sister. "It's cool behind the milk house and we won't see a thing."

Nellie agreed. As the autumn sky darkened and the pigs were herded towards their terrible end, the two sisters, one tall and one small, slipped over the hill behind the house. Sitting by a stream in the coolness of the evening, Lizzie showed her little sister how to make chains of stovepipe grass, and, as though by magic, from her apron pocket she produced two honey sandwiches on thick brown bread. As they ate, Lizzie tried to make her sister understand the importance of the annual pig kill.

"God made pigs for meat, Nellie. If we let them live, there would be pigs everywhere, and I know you wouldn't like that."

Nellie hesitated, put her sandwich down, and stared intently at the braided grass lying in her lap. "It's not that I love pigs so much, Lizzie. They are greedy brutes, it's true, but still I don't know why they should suffer. When a tree is cut, or grain, it doesn't squeal. Why can't God make it that way for pigs? Why must there be so much pain?"

Before Elizabeth could answer, a terrible, piercing cry came from the barnyard as the first animal was slaughtered. Nellie dropped her weaving and flung herself down face-first on the grassy bank. All Lizzie could do was pat her sister's hunched back and wait for the agonizing torment to pass.

"I'm through with being a Christian," hiccupped the wild-eyed Nellie when the tears and the mad squealing had, at last, subsided. "I don't love God. I'm not going to care for anything except having a good time. This world is a horrible place, Lizzie. Don't let the streams and the flowers fool you. I'll go to dances when I grow up and put hair-oil on my hair and stay out late. I'm through with Sunday school."

Wisely, Elizabeth Mooney let her youngest sister rail against the cruelty of the world. The wild, wicked words seemed to restore Nellie, and soon she agreed they should go back to the homestead. The wind was rising and a fingernail moon had appeared in the eastern sky. It was too dark to see the spilled pig blood or the butchering block, but the girls hurried past, not daring to breathe the smell of death.

In the house, all was calm and familiar. "There will be doughnuts tomorrow," said Lizzie, inhaling the pungent kitchen smell of freshly rendered lard.

"I won't eat one," said Nellie, firmly. "Or, at least not many."

∞

Although life at the homestead was often hard, it was typical of early settlement in Ontario. The Mooney land was in Sullivan Township along the pioneer road the government built to gain access to newly acquired Indian lands in Georgian County. Although resplendent with timbers, the land was not meant for cultivation, and after years of toil it produced only enough feed for chickens and a handful of cows. The garden kept the family fed, but when other items were needed, it was Letitia's butter and eggs that earned cash to buy the few small things the Mooneys could not make themselves.

This subsistence existence had a profound affect on Nellie's elder brothers, William and George. They quickly grew to realize the rocky Ontario farm wouldn't provide them a living. It could barely support their family, and both knew dividing the land to support a wife and their own children was unthinkable. At best the brothers might become farmhands for a more wealthy farmer. John Mooney's hard-scrabbled property held no future.

In 1878, when Nellie was almost five years old, her eldest brother William went to John and Letitia with the idea of heading West to seek a better fortune for himself. Like a wild creature attentive to a changing wind, Nellie was there, listening. An adventure hovered on the horizon!

∽

The Toronto *Globe* lay open on the pine table. William had marked these words:

"One hundred and sixty acres for ten dollars
as a homestead, and another one hundred
and six as a preemption for a moderate price.
You could plow a furrow a mile long and
never strike a stone!"

Although Nellie hadn't quite conquered her alphabet, she knew intuitively the article had something to do with the wonderful visitor, Michael, and William's dream. "Man-i-to-ba," she whispered under her breath, so her father wouldn't hear.

Michael Lowery, a neighbour, had come to the Mooney home yesterday. He was a giant of a man, marvellous in a Shaganappi coat fringed with doeskins and glass beads, all the colours in God's creation. It wasn't simply his coat that made Michael so exotic, but his red tuque and bandana, the box of moccasins he brought – which even Letitia had to admire – and his booming voice that filled up every space in the kitchen until Nellie wondered if the walls would explode with his excitement. Clinging to the edge of the room, Nellie watched and listened, fascinated, as Michael talked of his two years out West where there were no trees to cut, no stumps, no rocks, just prairie waiting for the plow. By Michael's side, William Mooney glowed as if it were his own shoulder guiding the effortless planting.

Nellie's brother was convinced Manitoba held more promise than Ontario. He, along with countless others, had succumbed to the seductive spell of rich western soil, unending sunshine, and cheap land calling out to those willing to claim it.

Nellie could tell by the look on her father's face that he wasn't convinced by Michael's stories. Big game, friendly Indians, hundreds of hectares without bush or stone, wild plums and cranberries spilling on the ground with no one to pick them – none of it seemed to touch John Mooney. He was sixty-six years old and the thought of a new start in a new land was daunting.

But Nellie knew her mother's interest was piqued. Although Letitia lapsed into her dismissive Dundee brogue with a curt – "Paper and pen refuses nothing" – Nellie caught her carefully studying the newspaper.

When George and Will had come home the week before with the smell of alcohol on their breath, there'd been hell to pay. Letitia had slammed pots and doubled the workload. That night Nellie had overheard a discussion – her father's low, easy tone and her mother's words, a furious, barely contained whisper: "No sons of mine will be known for frequenting the drinking parlours of Chatsworth, John. Perhaps it's time to think of their future. Maybe out West…" – and she'd lowered her voice so Nellie had to strain to hear. *Maybe out West.*

In the Mooney home the mythology of the Golden West grew as winter turned to spring and the days lightened and lengthened. William was never home. He'd rush through chores and hasten to the Lowery farm with barely a word to his siblings. George could tag along but Nellie was rarely invited despite her desperate pleas to hear the stories of "out West."

The more Western propaganda Will brought into the Mooney farmhouse, the more his dream edged toward reality. The Montreal *Gazette* called the West "The Land of Opportunity," and reports of settlement – four hundred Ontario settlers arriving at the same time in May 1878 and in that month alone collectively taking up over forty thousand hectares of prime farmland – filtered into the Chatsworth community.

"I'm sure we're going," Hannah told Nellie, as the two prepared for bed. "Mother's started another quilt and I've heard Arabella Cresine is coming to sew as soon as she's through with the Chartons' sewing."

"What about Papa?"

"You'll have to convince him, Nellie. He'll listen to you."

Dreams and questions floated through Nellie's imagination. Would they go West? Would Papa agree? What if they were attacked by Indians? Could she bring her dogs, Nap and Watch? And what about their cattle and the chickens? Would they have to be killed like the poor pigs? A thousand questions put Nellie to sleep that night, but the vision of an adventure, a new life, woke her up energized and excited the next morning.

Nellie found herself singing the chorus of a popular song as she fed the chickens: "So pack up your duds: say goodbye to yur ma, and try your luck farming in Man-i-to-bah." Saying goodbye to her ma was something Nellie thought she could manage. It wasn't often they saw eye to eye, and clashes of will were getting more and more frequent. *Hold your tongue. Stop acting the fool.* Letitia was strict and forthright, quite unlike John Mooney, the indulgent father who admired his youngest daughter's spunky attitude and laughed at her uncanny ability to mimic all the family, most of the neighbours, and a good percent of the townsfolk as well. Nellie knew she wouldn't be going anywhere without her beloved father.

☙

On a bright, windy day in late May, the decision was made. Nellie was watching her mother knead bread when the door flew open and William, ablaze in a red-faced fury, roared into the kitchen. "I'm done," he shouted. "I've had it." The only sound was the steady squeak of bread as Letitia broke the air bubbles inside the dough.

"Did the plow hit a stone, William? Are you hurt?" Letitia asked calmly.

"Yes, of course the plow hit a stone. There is no end to stones. But I'm through with stones, Mother. I quit. I'm going West."

And so, two days later, in the spring of 1879, nineteen-year-old William Mooney and his friend Neil Macdonald set off for Manitoba, determined to find land for their respective families. Nellie wept bitterly at the side of the road as the stagecoach to Owen Sound carried her brother away in a cloud of dust. Her mother, with her Old World reverence for the opinions of men, thought William's choice was fine. He'd promised a weekly letter, and though it grieved her to see the family split up, the prospect of a larger parcel of land in a new place was worth this small separation.

Nellie was sure of only two things: William had looked extraordinarily handsome in his new grey felt hat, and if anybody could, *he* could conquer the world. She had to speak to her father.

John Mooney had not gone up to the Garafraxa Road to see his eldest son off. He'd gone instead to the barn "to think on things awhile." Nellie found him there, in the sweet-smelling hay barn, drawing deeply on his pipe and lost in thought.

"I'm worried about the dogs, Papa," she said. "What shall we do with them when we go West?"

"Your Uncle Abner might take the brown spaniel, Nellie. Our playboy Nap is quite useless when it comes to rounding up the cows or chasing hawks, but he's a joyous pup and Abner might like him."

"But what about Watch? He's old and ugly. He never plays, never has any fun. Mother is the only one who likes him. What will become of him?"

"That dog has a stern sense of duty, Nell, not a bad thing in an animal and an even better thing in a person," replied John. "Old Watch needn't be so suspicious, grim, and cross with the world, and Nap might do well to learn some usefulness along with his playful ways."

He pulled Nellie up onto his knee and smiled, a bit sadly. "When Christ came to earth, he came to show us it's not impossible to be full of fun and fond of music, yet serious and earnest too. You, my bonny, would do well to combine the virtues of Watch with the playfulness of Nap."

"Because we're moving West, Papa?"

"Aye, because we'll need all the help we can get in our move West. And balance, Nellie, makes for peace."

၈၅

A year after his son left, John sold the Ontario property to William Crawford for a little over one thousand dollars. Letitia gave up her dower rights, sold the remaining stock, farm equipment, and the few extraneous household items she thought might not be needed in Manitoba. When all was in order and the May sunshine melted the snow, the family was ready to leave.

The Mooneys had almost sixteen hundred dollars. Much of that would go towards outfitting themselves in Winnipeg, in preparation for their foray into the true Canadian wilderness. William had kept his promise and written all about his findings. The boys, initially hired by the Winnipeg surveying party of Caddy and Huston, had quickly learned the scope of the new land. William ascertained most of the land in Southern Manitoba that wasn't held in reserve had already been sold to speculators. He also wrote of a great central plain beyond the Manitoba border where he and Macdonald had wintered in a crude log cabin in the Souris Valley. There, three miles up Oak Creek near the Souris River, William staked the Mooney claim: a half section for his father, a half section for himself and a quarter section for his brother George. To this patch of uninhabited prairie, the Mooneys pointed themselves on May 15, 1880, after they bade farewell to the farmhouse at Chatsworth. Like a great many settlers before them, the Mooneys chose the Great Lake port of Owen Sound as their departure point. Beyond Owen Sound was the frontier city of Duluth and beyond Duluth – well, that was what they were going to find out.

Nellie Mooney, a six-year-old sprite pressed against the lines at the very bow of the steamer, knew life had changed forever. But it was excitement that fuelled her and made her feet dance a happy pattern on the steel deck. In Manitoba they'd all have to pitch in, Mother had said, and Nellie was just as important as Hannah or Lizzie or George or Jack.

Nellie looked behind her. Storm clouds gathered on the eastern horizon of the lake but ahead, to the West, the spring sky was a marvellous, matchless blue.

"Manitobah" Settler's House and Red River Cart. The Red River Cart became synonymous with settlers making the trek west. Its large wheels were less likely to become mired in muck. A house similar to the one shown was the destination of the Mooney family in their western journey from Winnipeg to the Souris River.

# 2

## Roughing It

*"Why shouldn't I run with the boys?" – NLM*

The riverbank – world without end! Nellie loved it. The family had arrived two days before and were now camped at the junction of two great rivers, the Assiniboine and the Red. The canvas tent was up and Letitia was washing absolutely everything. Feather quilts hung from bushes, to dry under the blue bowl of sky.

Two nights ago, weary beyond words, the family had ended up spending a night sleeping on the floor of the Browse Hotel across the Red River from St. Boniface. There wasn't a room in town, and Nellie secretly hoped a friendly innkeeper would direct them to a stable just like Mary and Joseph in Bethlehem. No such luck. In the telling light of morning, Letitia hustled them out of the Browse so fast Nellie didn't have time to look around. Why call it the Browse if not allowed to browse? When her mother paid the bill – fifteen dollars – her mouth was pinched so tight Nellie thought she might be holding pins between her lips.

But the canvas tent city was glorious. There were settlers everywhere, hundreds of squatters buzzing with excitement. *Did you know...? Have you heard...?* Conversations about land, about Indians, about wolves and farming and winter, all these set against the to-ing and fro-ing of sidewheeler and propeller boats, the constant activities of the rivers. For Nellie it was paradise.

William arrived the next morning with his own stories. Wrestling with sleep next to the billowing canvas, Nellie strained to hear of her brother's adventures at the confluence of the Assiniboine and the Souris. "It was so cold frost split the trees in two. They opened with a pistol crack. The wolves howled and both my ponies died with frost upon their lungs..."

∞

Letitia and the children rented a house in St. James, about eight kilometres from Winnipeg, while John and his two elder sons went ahead to start house building. Staying behind would have been unbearable for young Nellie had it not been that Jack also had to stay behind "to be the man of the house."

Both sides of the splintered family were far from idle that summer. Letitia planted a huge garden behind the St. James house in order to provide vegetables for the coming winter, and she kept a close eye on her children, at one point forbidding Nellie from playing with the roving gang of Métis children that seemed to populate the riverbanks of their new neighbourhood.

"But why can't I play?" Nellie moaned. "They are allowed all the freedom in the world while we're like ponies tied to the fence of a little yard." Letitia, who later confessed to John she was uncomfortable with "the jet-black eyes and high cheek-bones" found there, remained firm, and the children had to content themselves with dreams of greater freedom once they reached Will's promised land, still more than two hundred kilometres to the West.

The single consolation for Nellie was Sir Donald A. Smith's manor house next door. After dark, she and Hannah would steal out to their second-storey balcony to watch the carriages come and go. They made up elaborate stories about humble fur traders, pretty maidens, and uppity British lords. The adventurer, never the wealthy ruler, always won the heart of the lady. Hannah played the trader who, just at the precise moment in the imaginary drama, would snap his handkerchief out of his pocket to dry the tears of his beloved. Nellie made up most of the dialogue, and, with wild applause, was the biggest fan of her own dramas.

∽

In early September 1880 – once the men had returned and Letitia had preserved the bounty of her garden – the final leg of the journey began. Two canvas-covered wagons pulled by oxen, a small black cow named Lady, and a sure-footed pinto pony rolled out onto Portage Road on a sunny Monday morning. Letitia, who liked to keep her hawk eye on the entire procession, travelled at the rear of the caravan. Nellie and her siblings walked with their mother, ran ahead with their father, or rode on the back of the wagons. At the side of the trail on the third day Nellie noted a small grave marker. *Linda*, it read. A cross was etched beside the name, and while Letitia pretended not to see, Nellie and Hannah and Lizzie talked of nothing else.

With the forlorn spirit of little dead Linda bravely leading them, the girls told themselves to ignore the Old Testament plagues of mosquitoes and the sea of mud, black and greasy, that slurped and licked at the wagon wheels and threatened to swallow alive their trusty oxen. The Mooneys made two stopovers, one at High Bluff, where they purchased a Red River cart made without a single nail, and the other at Poplar Point, where they visited former Chatsworth neighbours. These stopovers broke the long journey up, but it was still a full fourteen days before they saw William's oft-talked-of Sand Hills.

George, who had been left at the new homestead, ran to greet his family and scooped Nellie into his arms. Nuzzling her face into her older brother's neck, Nellie smelled woodsmoke and sweat and buckskin overlaid by the sweet aroma of sage. As soon as she saw the log house with the prairie grass thatched roof, she knew life would be good here. The house stood on high ground circled by a running stream and edged with clumps of willows. Will had found them a place with a view. Away to the south, hazy in the distance, the Tiger Hills stood, and to the Northwest, the high shoulder of the Brandon Hills looked dark blue and compellingly mysterious. Nellie squirmed from her brother's embrace and ran to explore. Freedom thrummed in every footfall. The prairie echoed with possibilities.

∞

Yesterday, when the temperature rose from 35 to 30 below, Nellie's father and brothers broke through the creek ice and hauled water to the cabin. A coating of ice, a few centimetres thick on the outer logs of the house, helped keep out the whistling wind, but the cold still came through some of the poorly chinked timbers. Today would be another interminably long day inside. Snow had fallen continuously since October, and walking outside was treacherous. With visions of a child floundering in chest-deep snow, Letitia had kept the girls in. Only the men, always only the men, could go out. Sharing a single pair of snowshoes, they continually hauled water and wood to the cabin. Letitia kept the wood stove glowing red.

Just before Christmas came a break in the snow. Nellie begged to go out. "I'll just check on Lady," she said. "I'll keep to the path." Letitia agreed, but before she turned from the door a piercing shriek rose from the paddock. Nellie had discovered Lady, the family cow, dead in the snow. With her horns trapped in a poplar-pole fence, the cow had fallen and apparently broken her neck. The cold finished her off. Nellie stood rigid, staring at the stiff body of the cow. The sight was horror beyond tears, but when they came, with great gushing sobs, the teardrops froze on her cheeks until Lizzie rushed her indoors.

While Lady's death meant the end of butter and milk for the Mooneys, it also shattered something in Nellie that could never be replaced. A sense of security. She couldn't put her feelings into words, but in her heart she recognized the grim possibility that a sinister, unseen presence could cause disaster to darken even the brightest day.

John took the meat from the cow, but because the ground was frozen solid, he could not bury the carcass. He dragged Lady's remains from sight and left her for the wolves, which often appeared around the cabin in the evening. That night was horror-filled for little Nellie, who imagined hundreds of snarling, snapping, hungry ghouls coming to gnaw on the bones of the cow. Inside the cabin, Nellie matched the pack's howls of hunger with wails of grief and terror. "We brought her all the way out here, just to die," she cried, refusing comfort. "Poor Lady. Poor, poor Lady. What will become of us? Will we be feed for the wolves as well?"

"Hush, child," cautioned Letitia. "You'd do well not to speak like that. Times will be hard enough without you wishing them so."

Letitia's words were prophetic. As bitter January gave way to a colder February, fourteen-year-old Elizabeth, Nellie's much-loved oldest sister and the one who often comforted the small girl when her imagination ran wild, became gravely ill. Nothing Letitia tried could stop the fever raging through Lizzie's body. The child's jaw locked, her unseeing eyes gazed at the thatched roof of the cabin, and she eventually lapsed into a coma.

Nellie, convinced her sister would go the way of Lady, flung herself down on the raw lumber floor. "Please, God, I will believe in you again if only you let Lizzie live. I will. I will. I promise to believe." Letitia, who had exhausted all her home remedies and medical knowledge, was desperate. "I can't save her, John. What have we done coming so far, so cruelly far. What's money? What's land? What comfort can we have when we remember this, our best girl dying for want of a skilled hand?" Letitia sank to the floor next to Nellie. "Lord, have mercy."

A day later, after nearly six weeks with no visitors, a snowshoe-clad stranger showed up at the door of the Mooney cabin. Reverend Thomas Hall, the Methodist minister from the settlement of Millford, brought medicine and the skills to administer it. Nellie felt she could kneel at his feet and worship him. To her it seemed as if the man were an angel sent directly from God. Angel or not, three days after his arrival, Lizzie began to recover. Nellie's faith was restored. God had heard their pleas. A miracle had happened.

∞

Although isolation and loneliness proved difficult through the first winter, the Mooneys were not alone in their adventure. A number of pioneer communities sprang up around them in the early 1880s, and by the end of their first winter they found neighbours, the Naismith family, living a mere five kilometres downstream. This was heartening to the Mooneys, who felt that the presence of neighbours meant the wilderness could be beaten back, the wolves kept at bay, and a new civilization founded.

In 1881, their homestead in the Souris River Valley became part of Manitoba when the province's boundaries were extended. In 1882, the same year the Canadian Pacific Railway (CPR) reached Brandon, the Mooneys built a new house with three proper bedrooms. They cultivated 324 hectares of farmland and purchased livestock, including two new cows, a few ducks and turkeys, some pigs and a flock of laying hens. Around their new home they planted a row of Manitoba maples and a variety of flower seeds brought from Ontario. Millford, eight kilometres away at the junction of Oak Creek and the Souris River, grew to a bustling centre, and to Nellie's joy, a schoolhouse was under construction at Northfield, little more than three kilometres from the Mooney homestead.

"I have trapped thirteen mink and Jack has only nine," boasted Nellie to her sister after she finished tanning her last hide and tacking it with the others to the inside of the barn door. It was the spring of 1883 – the second spring after the house was built, the last glorious summer of freedom, when Nellie and her siblings ran wild on a prairie filled with buttercups and wild peas.

"You claim you have to check your traps every time there's a dish to do or a rug to shake," scolded Hannah. "Don't think we don't see, Nellie."

Often absent for indoor chores, Nellie had one primary responsibility: to make sure the henhouse door remained latched. The winter before, a weasel had slit the throats of twenty-six hens, and the Mooneys' new neighbours had given a chicken shower in June to help the family rebuild their flock. Nellie jokingly noted each of the four gift hens resembled its donor. She named them after the neighbour ladies and clucked and called to them when she spread their feed. Letitia was not impressed. "The Christian names of respectable married women are not to be lightly bandied about a farmyard, Nellie. Just mind the latch and check the door each night before bed."

While Nellie's aversion to killing animals wouldn't allow her to delight in the number of pelts she had acquired, she easily revelled in beating Jack, and this sibling rivalry completely erased Letitia's chore from her mind. She awoke that night sick with guilt. The henhouse door! Were the chickens dead? Had they felt the weasel's tooth? Filled with dread at what she might find, she crept out in the darkness in her thin cotton nightgown and stumbled over something warm and soft at the henhouse door. Her dog Nap lay like a sentry in front of the small wooden structure. Guiltily, Nellie closed the latch and ruffled the head of the faithful dog.

Less than a week later, while working the fields, Nellie saw Nap and another black dog leaping and biting at the tails of the cattle. This was an unforgivable deed. Nellie knew cows with docked tails would bring very little when sent to auction. There was no getting around it. Nap's fate, should she tell, would be a bullet to the head.

The family was gathered around the table when Nellie told her first lie. It was the black dog acting alone, she said. Nap was by her side when they watched the neighbour's black cur nip the tails of the cattle.

"I'll speak to them tomorrow and have the animal put down," said John, who had seen the bloodied stumps of tail and asked if anyone had witnessed what happened.

Jack spoke up. "They'll probably say the dog was home all day. What's to stop them saying it was Nap that did the damage? No one saw it but Nellie and they know she's so crazy about Nap she might lie to save him."

"Now, that's enough," interrupted Letitia. "There isn't a person in this neighbourhood who wouldn't take Nellie's word."

Choking with humiliation and shame, Nellie sat, glad for the darkness of the kitchen but certain her family could hear the beating of her heart. In recounting the painful story years later, Nellie confessed, "I was utterly miserable; made moreso by the fact that my story was not doubted. I had a good name and had thrown it away."

Unfortunately the lie had its own ramifications. When Nap was gored by a boar later that summer, Nellie suffered the agony of remorse. She had spared the dog's life and marred her own conscience, only to have him suffer horribly. Was it my lie that made Nap suffer such agony at the end of his life, she wondered? Or is it just another tragedy, like the pigs going to slaughter and the wolves eating Lady?

When Letitia questioned the dark rings under Nellie's eyes, she admitted she'd sat up half the night nursing her dog and pondering the uneven quality of life. "I couldn't put it into words but some glimmering of life's plan swept across my mind. Sorrow and joy, pain and gladness, triumph and defeat were in that plan, just as day and night, winter and summer, cold and heat, tears and laughter. We couldn't refuse it. We must go on."

Nap survived his brush with death and Nellie her burden of guilt, but the henhouse incident and the struggle with her conscience marked Nellie as a contemplative child, quick to analyse and justify the pain and pleasures of life. While optimism ultimately defined her personality, it sprang from many a dark night of the soul.

Putting her head against the warm flank of one of the new cows and hearing the steady thrum of the milk in the pail, Nellie knew her mother was right: hard work would save her. "I'm glad for chores," she whispered to the milking-cow, which stood patient and dumb at her side. "This is life's remedy. Not philosophy or explanations. Just this. Work!"

∞

Incidents on the farm in Nellie's early years, before her formal education began in earnest, shaped and formed her personality as much as schooling did later. When

her brothers and father came back to the farmhouse at
the end of the day and complained bitterly about the
forty-kilometre trek to the nearest elevator in Brandon
and the CPR monopoly on grain collection, Nellie listened intently. When government tariff protection on
Canadian farm machinery hindered the harvest of
1883, Nellie was incensed along with her father. Why
was the machinery from the western United States so
much more expensive than the machinery from
Ontario? And why did Manitoba farmers have to buy
Canadian machines when it became apparent the har-
vesters from Ontario weren't up to the job? Last summer's breakdown of the family binder, purchased from
Ontario the year before, had cost the family precious
harvest days, and part of the crop was still in the field
when the frost came. Was it their fault the mechanical
parts never arrived on time? What did Ottawa know of
the reality of Western farming?

∞

"I won't be joining," said John Mooney of the fledgling
Manitoba Farmers' Protective Union, a loose organization of Western farmers wanting provincial control over
public land, an end to the CPR monopoly, railway
branch lines built to centres of commerce, and the lowering of tariffs on equipment. "I understand what it is
they want, but I cannot understand why they can't be
thankful for what we have now, compared to what we
had back there. Don't they remember?" At seventy,
Nellie's father was slowing down. The battles of the
future – unions, provincial autonomy, and tariffs –

would have to be fought by his sons. And, it turned out, by his daughters.

∽

Nellie and Hannah walked towards the Millford fairgrounds on the outskirts of town. It was July 1,1883 and the second annual community picnic was underway. Folks from as far away as Oak Creek and Brandon Hills were gathered under a cloudless sky. A brass band could be heard playing "Rule Britannia," and as the girls crested the hill they could see a baseball game in full swing.

"I hope there is chocolate again," said Hannah, remembering the exotic foods of '82.

"I'm going to enter the three-legged race and the sack race this year," said Nellie.

Hannah's brow furrowed. "You can't. Your leg might show."

"And what if it does?" said Nellie, disdainfully. "It's a perfectly good leg. If they're worried about my skirt flapping, why, I'll take it off and race in my underwear."

Hannah gasped and started to laugh. She knew the Victorian standards of dress and decorum for women weren't likely to be overthrown by Nellie or anyone else. Still, Nellie was a cheeky girl with an unreasonable determination. Hannah didn't want her sister to scandalize the community.

"Let's watch the slow ox races," she said, by way of distracting her younger sister. "Our Jake is entered. He won last year. He's a patient, placid fellow and I heard Jimmy Sloan is the rider."

"Oh, look," cried Nellie, ignoring Hannah and pointing across the field. "There's Mrs. Dale and her new baby. Oh, can't we go see the baby, Hannah? Please? The race won't start for a few minutes and I want to hold the baby."

Hannah nodded and Nellie was off. Several women were gathered around a carriage. By the time Hannah reached the group, Nellie had the carriage in hand and was wheeling it to the sidelines so she could get a better view of the ox race. The baby was asleep, just a bump in a blanket, but Nellie looked enormously proud and happy.

"They're starting."

At the top of the field, four beasts moved across the start line, towards the girls. Jake plodded along, steady and slow.

"He's going to win again. Good Jake. Slow Jake," applauded Hannah.

Suddenly the Mooney ox gave a startled bellow and began to gallop like a mad creature straight towards Nellie and the baby carriage. A horrified silence fell on the crowd, and Nellie's heart turned cold with terror. Jake was gasping and frothing at the mouth. His white hide was stained crimson – blood, bright and sickly fresh, ran down his flank. Jimmy Sloan had used spurs on the patient ox. He had been drinking alcohol, and he had used spurs against Jake.

The rest of the day was a blur. Mrs. Dale, white-faced with panic, grabbed the handle of the carriage and marched her baby out of harm's way. Indignant voices were raised. Who brought alcohol to the picnic?

There was a dance that night, but Nellie hadn't the heart to attend. William reported that drinking got out of control. Old grievances became inflamed, heads were smashed, noses broken, and at least one man had his ear chewed. This first contact with public drunkenness marked Nellie deeply. Later, she wrote of that night: "Some think of how drink loosens the tongue and drives out self-consciousness and makes for good fellowship when people meet. I think of none of these things. I remember a good day spoiled; peaceful neighbours suddenly growing quarrelsome. I feel again a helpless blinding fear, and see blood dyeing the side of a dumb beast."

Pulling her feather comforter over her eyes, Nellie made a vow to herself. She wanted to be part of the men's world of decision-making, but never, never, did she want to partake in the evils of alcohol. In that moment before sleep she envisioned a two-headed beast. One head shouted that all women should remain silent and subservient, and its nasty twin, with the ugly blast of liquor on its breath, roared agreement. Nellie hunkered deeper into her bed. She quickly imagined herself standing against the weaving, dancing dragon. In her hand she gripped a sword. She would slay the two-headed monster.

The following year, the July 1st picnic was cancelled.

To Nellie, the town of Brandon is a bustling city in 1890. A shop
selling books is the main draw for the literature-hungry schoolgirl.

The Winnipeg Normal School educates Nellie
in the ways of the rural classroom.

# 3

## *Reading and Freedom*

*"No one knows what books can mean except those of us who have been hungry for them."*
*– NLM*

"I think they were neglected," said Nellie. "Nobody listened to them or cared about what they wanted. Settlement was forced on them."

"But they were half-bloods, Nellie, already intermarried" argued Hannah. "Killing North West Mounted Police, who came to take care of things, only made it worse."

"But remember how we were frustrated when nobody in Ontario listened to us? The Métis must have felt the same way, only worse, because they suddenly had to obey a government who they knew nothing about, and who knew even less about them."

Nellie and Hannah were hoeing potatoes and planning their written defence of the Métis in the Northwest Rebellion. News of native insurrection in Saskatchewan's Battleford district had wafted back to Manitoba, and Riel and his men were very much the topic of the day, particularly at Frank Schultz's one-room school, which both girls had begun to attend eighteen months earlier. Jack, fourteen at the time, had opted not to go to school, and he quickly took on a man's role on the farm. Today, in the livestock barn to check the feet of the pony, he kept half an ear on the conversation from the garden.

The notion of his sisters having strong opinions and daring to write them down went totally against tradition. Jack told his parents the thrust of Nellie and Hannah's paper, and as he fully expected, its anti-British sentiment troubled Letitia.

"Dangerous seeds are being sown by this German fellow," she said to John. "The Germans have no love for British institutions, and I fear this Mr. Schultz is undermining our children's respect for authority. I often wonder if there be any value in teaching girls at all. I'll have to go before the trustees, John."

When Nellie heard this news, her heart sank. Mr. Schultz had taught her to read in less than three months. He was a wonderful teacher, always fair. He didn't like Annie Adams more than Nellie or think Annie smarter just because she had a cashmere dress and ribbons in her hair. He was a homesteader, just like them. How could her mother threaten his job?

John interjected, "Leave it, Lettie. Maybe there's something to the girls' argument."

"John Mooney. I'm surprised at you. I'll go to his home on Pelican Lake and speak to him myself, if need be. I won't have the girls talk like traitors. They're in the league of Guy Fawkes with their paper on Riel and the rights of half-breeds."

Nellie and Hannah exchanged glances. Their mother, steeped in Victorian traditions and prejudices, was on the warpath. No one was safe.

In mid-December 1884 Mr. Schultz arrived at the Mooney home to have a goodwill visit with John and Letitia. But history would not be turned. On April 24, 1885 the guns roared at Fish Creek. That spring, troops from Ottawa came through Brandon on their way west to Saskatchewan. In July, the battle was fought at Batoche, and Riel captured. The uprising was squelched with brutal bloodshed. On November 7, 1885 in the cold jail yard of the Mounted Police barracks in Regina, Louis David Riel was hanged for treason.

The news came to Nellie by way of the *Brandon Times* and the Montreal *Family Herald*. The reality of the event shocked the children into silence. Mr. Schultz spoke of martyrdom and bitterness in the Métis and First Nations communities, while at home, Letitia pursed her lips and said nothing. In her mind, justice had been served.

Nellie could not believe a dishevelled rider hadn't galloped up to the gallows at the last moment with a reprieve from the King. Her fantasy was thwarted. Riel had died. She read of riots in the streets of Montreal and Prime Minister Sir John A. Macdonald's effigy being burned in a public square.

"Books always talk about kings and rulers and how they make their decisions," Nellie confided to her sister, shortly after Mr. Schulz and Letitia had gone head-to-head over the Métis issue. "I am more interested in the people who aren't in the books. I want to know what the decisions of the rulers mean in real life." Real life was all too clear as Nellie recalled the children she'd played with on the shore of the Red River, almost a decade before. Their kin were the ones slain on the banks of the South Saskatchewan. This was a lesson in reality written in blood.

∽

Although the Mooneys were doing well in Manitoba, they were not wealthy. After years of making do on the Ontario property, thrift was second nature to Letitia, and Nellie wrote of her mother's "acid little economies." In her six years at school Nellie wore first her own, then Hannah's, and finally Lizzie's, green coat. Letitia had sewn the three of them, identical except in size, from the same bolt of cloth

"It's as though the awful thing will not wear out," bemoaned Nellie as Letitia straightened the lapel of the despised garment before Nellie left for school. "Annie Adams thinks it's the same coat year after year. She wears store-boughten things and all of mine are made-over or twice worn."

"That's enough, Nellie," cautioned Letitia. "I'll put a pair of bloomers on your bed. I've just finished them and they've not been worn by a soul."

"But no one *sees* my bloomers," responded Nellie.

"I should hope not."

When Nellie returned from class that day, the newly made bloomers were, indeed, on Nellie's bed. But what bloomers! They were bright red, a screeching, scarlet pair of underwear that had been accidentally dyed with the rag rugs.

"I can't wear them," cried Nellie. "Annie Adams will laugh herself sick."

But wear them she did. The humiliation of the red bloomers, coupled with the shapeless green coat, kept Nellie glued to the books rather than racing around the schoolyard. The indirect result of her fear that other children would glimpse her pantaloons and know her mother's frugal nature was her success as a student and Mr. Schulz's suggestion she consider a career in teaching. "You're an independent thinker, Nellie, you work hard, and teaching is an honourable profession."

∞

Books, to Nellie, were like logs to a fire. She read indiscriminately. And, fortunately for the hungry young mind, books, periodicals, magazines, and assorted articles came her way from a most unlikely source.

A British woman, Miss M.E. Breasted, did her part for the farflung Commonwealth by sending out packets of reading material to the settlers of the Canadian West. One family in each of Manitoba's new townships received Miss Breasted's anonymous charity four times a year, and few were as grateful as Nellie. She read *Ivanhoe, Swiss Family Robinson, Life of Livingston, Twenty Thousand Leagues Under the Sea, Evelina, The Arabian Nights*, Longfellow's poetry, Milton's classical works, the Bible, church magazines, *A Girl's Own Annual*, advertising material for farm equipment, the backs of calendars, anything she could get her hands on.

Still, what she most anticipated were the romantic serial novels that came with the Montreal *Family Herald*. The five miles to Millford to collect the post was never a long journey for Nellie, for her destination would hold new reading material, and nothing, absolutely nothing, could beat the freedom of escaping into another world through stories. Sometimes, particularly after a mother/daughter confrontation, books were Nellie's only solace.

After a particularly bad scrap, Nellie curled up in her small bedroom under the eaves to nurse her wounded pride. She put aside her much-thumbed copy of Mary Jane Holmes's *Meadow Brook* and thought of her own funeral. The heroine of the story, like Nellie, was the youngest of her family, a bitterly misunderstood child with a heart of gold. She decided to lie on the dewy grass, caught cold, and died, mostly to spite her unfeeling family. It was a grand idea. "Even Mother would be sorry then," mused Nellie. "And Jack. He will cry bitterly, 'Our Nell was too good to live.' Oh, I should so like to see him repent."

But, reasoned Nellie, going back to her book, Letitia always countered colds with mustard plasters and goose oil. "Instead of dying, I'm going to become a famous author," she told Nap, who thunked his tail in amicable agreement. "I'll not be a dreary housewife, with babies and washing and food to prepare for menfolk. I'll have money from my books and I'll be able to pay servants."

Nellie grievance against her mother and brother sprang from her first trip to Brandon, when she was just a few months shy of her twelfth birthday

The bitter incident happened at the Black Creek stopping house, halfway along the almost forty-five-kilometre trip to the nearest grain elevator. Jack, nearly seventeen by then, reined the team of horses in for water, and Nellie, eyes glowing with excitement, followed Letitia into the house for a cup of tea with one of the women who lived at the stopping house, Mrs. Corbett.

Later, back in the sleigh, Jack complained that Nellie was showing off, particularly to the large group of men who were eating their midday meal at the stopping house. "I felt cheap seeing you act in such a bold way," he told his sister, in no uncertain terms.

Nellie looked confused. "Jack, I did nothing but pour tea for the men. The boy who was supposed to do it was slow and clumsy. You saw for yourself."

Jack would have none of it. In his mind, his sister had acted out of turn. Letitia agreed. "Must you be so forward, child?" she chided, as the sleigh jogged along the trail. "You'll have to learn to restrain yourself, Nellie, particularly in the company of strangers. Do you think men want to see a chatty woman full of herself and her own opinions? Think, child."

Fuming, Nellie sulked the rest of the way to Brandon. She had simply been helping out when help was needed. Why must women constantly stand aside, deferring to men, when women were obviously more capable?

Stewing over her mother's and brother's unfair response to her act of kindness, Nellie could barely wait to get away from the repressive regime of family. Freedom, she thought, would be leaving the sleigh behind, turning her back on her critics, and making her own way in Brandon. But she was not yet of age.

In the city, after the household necessities were purchased, Nellie went to a bookstore. The sight of so many books, all for the asking, calmed her a little, but Jack's comments still made her cheeks flame with anger. Bold, indeed! She'd show them what bold was. Why, she would teach school and make her own money and write books in her spare time. She fingered the single dollar in her pocket. Today she might have one dollar, but soon enough she'd have a lot more. If people didn't like a girl who was too quick with her tongue or too ready with an answer, they would just have to get used to it, or have no acquaintance with her.

∞

Nellie Mooney knew before she reached her teens that she was not meant to stand passively by while the world roared past. The hustle and bustle of Brandon was thrilling and she loved the bright lights of the small city. She wanted to venture out into a wider world, and books and learning would be her ticket. Her sister

Lizzie married a farmer. George and Will also had their own farms, and their wives were producing the first batch of John and Letitia's grandchildren. Nellie was determined to take a different route.

In July 1889, Nellie learned she had passed the entrance exams for Normal School with top marks. A way to escape from the farm into her dazzling future suddenly opened up, but the reality of leaving her family and moving to Winnipeg spurred Nellie to look at her surroundings and her parents with fresh eyes.

Her father was becoming increasingly frail, and Letitia seemed saddened by Nellie's determined departure. Recognizing she would soon be on her own, Nellie's view of her mother softened; she was able to admit her judgments of Letitia unfair.

When she wrote her memoirs years later, Nellie observed that her mother had consistently displayed strength of character, unwavering kindliness, and a sharp, almost sardonic wit. These characteristics, combined with John's gentleness and humour, would manifest themselves in the person Nellie was to become. Nellie would eventually achieve the balance John had recommended, but for a hot-headed teenager, it was a long time in the winning.

$\infty$

"I want my students to behave because they want to please me, not because I demand it of them," Nellie confided to her roommate and fellow student teacher, Lillian Dale, following a Baptist church meeting the girls attended three months into their Winnipeg term.

"It's the same principle that troubles me about tonight's talk. I want to serve God because I love Him, not because I'm afraid He'll punish me."

Lillian and Nellie were on their way back to the school housed in the Stobart Block on Winnipeg's Portage Avenue. Although the December evening was chilly the girls walked because the price of a horse-drawn streetcar was dear, and two months of classes, including trial teaching in real classrooms, stretched before them. Just as they were about to turn into Richardson's bookstore to warm themselves by the heater, a fancy cutter passed, kicking up slush. Nellie caught a glimpse of a man in a brown buffalo-robe with red-flannel scalloped edges.

"Did you see his companion, Nellie?" asked Lillian, suddenly distracted from their conversation about discipline in the classroom. "She had the daintiest fur boots."

"Someday we'll be able to buy boots like that, Lillian," assured Nellie, turning into the warm haven of the store. "But I hope I will always prefer books over boots. Books can take you places little fur boots will never step."

∽

Along with her flare for the dramatic and her natural inclination to take the limelight, Nellie was developing her own moral, social, and political code. She dallied with the fundamentalism of the Baptist church, but it was John Mooney's Methodists who provided her with a moderate religious education, one that emphasized application of Christian principles to everyday life. That, combined with Nellie's passion for social justice and equality, marked her as a progressive Liberal. She knew the value of discourse and prompted her fellow students to debate the benefits of marriage contracts, the evils of liquor companies in a free enterprise society, and the value of domestic cooperatives for working women. In short, Nellie loved to stir the pot.

In early February 1890, her term at Normal School ended. With high ideals and a vision for a better world dancing in her head – and, more importantly, a licence to teach grasped in her hand – Nellie Mooney went back to the Millford farm to visit her family. She was sixteen years old and she felt the world was, at last, hers for the taking.

Nellie Letitia Mooney, schoolmarm and social activist, at age 19.

# 4

## *All the World, a Stage*

*"I wanted to write, and how could I write unless I lived and felt, and sorrowed, and living was dangerous." – NLM*

"You're too young."

"I'm sixteen, Mother"

"Nellie, I know how old you are. How far away is it?"

"Hazel School, near Manitou."

"Where will you stay?"

"The superintendent will board me with a family called the Hornsbergs. It's all arranged."

And so, on August 16 1890, with her "whole life" in a beautiful tin trunk, her second-class teaching certificate

in hand, and her mother's words *Listen instead of talk,
Admit what you don't know*, and *You're always welcome
back home*, ringing in her ears, Nellie waved goodbye to
her family and caught the Wawanesa train for Somerset,
more than one hundred kilometres east of the Mooney
farm. The mysterious Mr. Hornsberg, a trustee for the
Hazel School, was to meet Nellie and take the new
teacher back to his farm, a further twenty kilometres
from Somerset.

Alone on the platform, with the rhythmic beat of
the disappearing train still vibrating on the rails, Nellie
gazed bleakly at her trunk, now looking small and insuf-
ficient next to the vast bush surrounding her. Not a soul
in sight. Not a barn! Not even a haystack! Nellie waited,
perched on her trunk, while mosquitoes danced across
her face. So this was freedom. She began to feel afraid.
Then she remembered the three oranges, a farewell gift
from the storekeeper in Wawanesa. How could anyone
with three oranges be downcast?

A man appeared on a buckboard. Red-faced and
sweating, he asked Nellie if anyone got off the train.

"Yes, I did."

The man's brows knit together. "I was expecting to
meet the teacher of our school, and I'll bet my bottom
dollar she's changed her mind," he grumbled. "These
lady teachers are so unpredictable."

"Too bad," replied Nellie saucily. "I was expecting
to meet a trustee, but it seems he forgot to come." She
grinned and held out her hand. "Mr. Hornsberg. I am
Nellie Mooney, your new teacher."

∽

The Hazel school was typical of its day: one room dominated by a blackboard, a map of the world, and a pot-bellied wood stove. Forty students, some as old as Nellie, filed into the schoolhouse her first day. An early frost had nearly destroyed most crops, and instead of having to help with the harvest, children were able to come to school. Dividing so many pupils into grades, devising a seating plan, learning their names, and handing out timetables and books was the most Nellie accomplished the first day. She felt defeat nipping at her ankles.

Fortunately, the family she boarded with had two children in Hazel School. Esther Hornsberg, who was Nellie's age, provided much needed moral support.

"It will be a fine year, Nell," she encouraged. "We'll all help out with the little ones and they can do sums while you give us our lessons."

And so it was. Nellie soon got into the habit of reading a much anticipated adventure story, *My Dogs in the Northland,* to the entire schoolhouse after morning prayer, and because quarrelling, scraps, and taunts ruled the schoolyard, Nellie declared physical play both morning and afternoon to burn off otherwise ill-directed energy.

She purchased a pigskin football, which quickly became emblematic of Hazel School. After ensuring each student agreed on the rules of the game, the entire school, both boys and girls, split into teams for a rough and tumble football match. Nellie, of course, hadn't the disciple to stand on the sidelines. Skirts flying, hair wild, she entered the game with gusto.

Rare is the teacher who can mix freely with students during recess and still maintain discipline in the classroom, but Nellie managed to do both. The football matches, she explained to the class, like the adventure story readings, were a privilege, a reward for accomplishment inside the schoolroom. The children both admired and respected their new teacher and worked hard to win her praise and keep their privileges intact.

School superintendent Edward E. Best noted that Hazel School No. 365 and young Miss Mooney were "progressing nicely," but others in the community, quick to judge, soon called Nellie's ways into question.

The football matches came to the attention of one of Manitou's most upstanding – and feared – citizens. Mrs. Jeffreys had no children to keep at home, and she owned her own driving horse, which, according to Nellie, added to the evil she could do. She frowned on girls playing football. And when she heard the teacher joined in this most unladylike activity, Jeffreys decided to report the unbecoming behaviour to the school authorities. Nellie, just seventeen but strong-willed, decided she would meet with Mrs. Jeffreys before her reputation was ruined by the meddling busybody.

☙

The Jeffreys' kitchen was warm with the smell of baking. Nellie and Mrs. Jeffreys were washing up after a pleasant enough meal, though Nellie noticed her imposing hostess wouldn't meet her eyes across the supper table. When Mr. Jeffreys went out, Nellie saw her chance. If there was ever to be a time to get Mrs. Jeffreys on side, it was now. She took a deep breath and launched her defence.

"It's horrible to hear young boys and girls throw hints and sneers across a school ground. I think the best way to stamp out nastiness is to give them something fresh and clean and thrilling to think about."

She glanced sidelong at Mrs. Jeffreys, who only pursed her lips, nodding. Refusing to be cowed, Nellie continued hurriedly, "A game of football ought to be more interesting than the story of how one man's father opened a registered letter and lost his job twenty years ago."

Mrs. Jeffreys blanched, her tea towel suspended in mid-air.

"Who said that?" she demanded, her face white. "That's a lie... It was all a mistake." Inadvertently Nellie had stirred up a bitter memory in her chief detractor. Her accidental blackmail shocked Mrs. Jeffreys into silence. Nellie quickly steered the conversation onto a different course and left the house as soon as convention and good manners would allow.

"I hit on something quite without meaning to," she explained to Esther as they whispered in their shared bed. "She was very angry, burning angry, but she contained it like smothering coals, and I'm fairly certain she won't be going anywhere near the school trustees." Her instincts proved correct, and Nellie's unorthodox method of behaviour management, the much loved football matches, continued unabated. A small battle, fought with plain talk, bluntness, and a mixture of good humour and common sense, proved Nellie the victor.

∞

Teaching in the free Common Schools of Canada towards the end of the nineteenth century was not all fun and games. Many of Nellie's students attended irregularly, depending on needs at the rural home-steads. School supplies were scarce and many families were too poor to buy the required supplies of slate and pencils. Children often stayed home in winter because they lacked boots or a coat or some other essential piece of clothing. Nellie, soft hearted and ever hopeful for her students, often found herself cutting down her old clothing to provide a shirt or a dress for a child in need.

More than such essentials, however, Nellie wished to provide her neighbours an escape from the drudgery of their everyday existence. She realized her students' parents had little to look forward to, consumed as they were with the burden of surviving. At least the children in school had some hope for the future, but what could she do to uplift the spirits of the parents pressed down by endless hours of work?

In late November Nellie had an idea. In the kitchen of the Hornsbergs' home, Nellie and Esther hatched their plan.

∞

"The school will host a massive Christmas feast. We'll have a concert with songs and carols. The older girls can recite poetry and we'll have a play. Esther, you can sing "Whispering Hope," and I'll help with harmonies. It will be a Christmas concert for the whole commu-nity." Typically Nellie became completely caught up in her vision, imagining how much happiness music and skits and poetry reading could bring to the hearts of people deprived of such things. Never one to shy away from centre stage, she cast herself in the role of the heroine in a comic skit she and Esther wrote, *Train to Morrow*.

Teacher and pupils banded together to rehearse and polish their performances. The concert ran on the eve of December 23, 1890, and as Nellie had predicted, the Hazel schoolhouse rocked with laugher, excitement, and applause until well after midnight.

∞

Heading home to her family on a westbound freight the next morning, Nellie recounted the evening's success to a group of dumbfounded trainmen. In an age where most women didn't speak to strange men, the outgoing Nellie Mooney regaled the group with stories . "We had such fun," she crowed, laughing in recollection. "Oh, if only you could have been there. It was a wonderful evening."

The conductor was only half listening for he was increasingly concerned about the weather. Shovelling coal into the round stove of the caboose, he tapped the coal bin as though to draw his passenger back to the present. "We want to get you home for Christmas, Miss, but a storm from the west is blowing fierce."

Indeed, a grey wall of whirling snow engulfed the freight and slowed the train to a snail's pace. Nellie produced sandwiches, cake, and candy, leftovers from the concert, and served them to the trainmen. As the night wore on, she offered her rendition of *Whispering Hope* and acted out all three parts of the school play in order to pass the time and translate the magic and wit of the concert to her new friends. Her captive audience was hours delayed by that ferocious blizzard, and it was Christmas afternoon when Nellie stepped onto the platform at Wawanesa to find Jack and the sleigh waiting patiently in the snow. Together they rode to the farm and the rest of the waiting family.

Letitia's delight at seeing her daughter safely home quickly turned to dismay as Nellie spoke of her adventure.

"You talked to the men?"

"Yes. And I sang. Later in the day, when we sat on a siding, I read a few chapters of *Lucille* out loud."

"And where did you sleep?" sputtered Letitia.

"They made up a small berth and covered me with a great fur coat. The conductor even brought a clean towel to cover the pillow. Wasn't that thoughtful? It was lovely chugging along the prairie, so warm and sleepy."

Aghast at her daughter's show-off behaviour, Letitia embarked on one of her standard lectures, but before the scolding gained momentum, John interjected. "I don't see the sin in it, Lettie. A little song and laughter can go a long way to bring balance to a bad situation."

∞

In the winter of 1891 Nellie made her first real attempt to win public support for the temperance movement.

She was convinced many good farmers were made poor by alcohol companies that supplied liquor as an antidote to despair, and many children lacked shoes because fathers spent cash at the Manitou bar. Men were neglecting their duties in order to indulge in destructive behaviour. Distillers and suppliers of alcohol became Nellie's target and she spoke out tirelessly against the evils of liquor. Her one supporter was the wife of Manitou's Methodist minister, Mrs. J.A. McClung.

A group of ten girls, hair in braids with the ends teased out in the fashion of the day, twittered and giggled in their room behind the choir loft. Officially, they were the Young Ladies Bible Class of the Manitou Methodist Church. Unofficially they were giddy teenagers awaiting their new Sunday school teacher, the minister's wife, recently arrived from Port Authur, Ontario.

When Annie E. McClung entered the classroom, Nellie was smitten. Her teacher was a beautiful, serene woman in her late forties. Her eyes, Nellie wrote, held "all the browns and greens and golds of the moss in the meadow brook at home when sunshine fell into its clear stream." She was wearing a smart brown cashmere dress with a smocked yoke and cuffs, and Nellie could barely keep her eyes off an iridescent moonstone brooch at Mrs. McClung's throat. Its purpose was to hold her linen collar in place, but to Nellie, the brooch reflected both beauty and purity.

"You sure had all the answers today, Nellie," said Esther Hornsberg after class dismissal. "I think you knew every coming and going of the Prodigal Son, and what it all meant, as well. I'm certain the new minister's wife was impressed."

"She is the only woman I should like to have for a mother-in-law," Nellie responded, oblivious to Esther's gentle teasing.

"Oh, according to Mother, she has two sons."

Nellie's eyes widened.

"But," laughed Esther, "they are only ten and fourteen years old."

Nellie was not to be deterred. "When I am fifty-three and the eldest boy fifty, no one will notice three small years," she replied.

∽

In McClung, Nellie found a new role model, a woman whose feelings about temperance were as strong as her own. Mrs. McClung also introduced Nellie to the cause of suffrage for women, a concept Nellie knew but had never heard articulated. Before she completed her term at Hazel School and moved into town to teach at the Manitou School, Nellie knew Mrs. McClung as an advocate, friend, and newfound mentor. What she didn't know, when the McClungs invited her to board at their home, was that the Reverend and Mrs. J.A. McClung had a third son, an older son.

Robert Wesley McClung was a student at the Toronto College of Pharmacy, and the summer he was nineteen he came and worked in the Manitou drugstore. Nellie decided it was time to get a look at the "red-haired McClung boy."

Wearing her best dark green dress with the military braid and brass buttons, her hair clean and lightly waved by curling papers the night before, Nellie set off after school on one of the Hornsbergs' horses. Her mandate was clear. She wanted to meet Wes McClung face-to-face.

"I am looking for a fountain pen, please," she said to the tall, slim young fellow with clear blue eyes, regular features, and the flawless skin of his mother. "I want something of quality that will last."

With infinite patience, Wes McClung helped Nellie with her selection. As she purchased a beautiful Dorothy Dix pen, she produced her last three dollars with an opulent flourish and a wide smile for the red-haired clerk. Trotting back to the farm three miles from town, Nellie knew she had set something important in motion. For the first time in a long while, she was silent.

Nellie was at a quilting bee when next she met her future mother-in-law. A dozen women, including a fellow schoolteacher, were working on a massive down quilt, a Christmas gift for the Methodist manse. Talk turned to a petition Mrs. McClung and another lady were circulating. The petition asked that women be allowed to vote.

"Imagine!" said one woman, full of scorn. "It's an insult to our husbands to even consider the vote."

"And what is the wife of a minister doing meddling in politics? Shouldn't she be knitting for missions or organizing Sunday school recitals?" another asked.

Nellie was incensed. They were speaking about her mentor with such scorn. Before she could respond, a knock sounded at the door. The quilters bolted upstairs, leaving Nellie and her hostess to face two women standing patiently at the front door.

"We were hoping to share this important document with your guests, Mrs. Brown, but it appears they have gone," said Mrs. McClung, proffering the petition. "Perhaps you would like to sign for women to have a voice in provincial leadership?"

"I think not. I do not care to," said the hostess.

Nellie glanced at Mrs. McClung's face. A quiet dignity rested on the woman as she pretended not to notice the ruffling and crackling of barely suppressed laughter upstairs. "I'd like to sign," said Nellie. Her name on the petition stood second. Again, she knew something important had transpired.

∞

Teaching in Manitou, a town of approximately eight hundred people, was quite a different experience for Nellie. While the Hornsberg farm was only a few miles west of Manitou, and Nellie visited the Methodist church every Sunday, she had never lived in town before. Nellie quickly got involved in the cultural and religious life of the community. She established the Manitou "literary society" for regular programs of music, readings, debates, dialogues, and recitations. She also joined the Women's Christian Temperance Union (WCTU) and began preparing for her first-class teaching certificate.

Despite a hectic schedule of teaching, studying, and socializing, Nellie always found time to write. A faithful, though often sporadic, keeper of journals, she still dreamed of becoming an author, and once settled in Manitou she turned her hand to writing short fiction. While much of that early writing has been lost, some remains. It is considered full of promise, as unsophisticated, fresh, and idealistic as the young schoolteacher herself.

∞

In January 1893, while Nellie was home for Christmas vacation, John Mooney died at the age of eighty-one. Grief and a deep sense of unshakeable regret seized Nellie. In the familiar farmhouse kitchen, two days after John was laid to rest behind the small Methodist church, Nellie poured tea for her mother and her sisters. Great tears fell from her eyes, landing plop, plop, on the table that had witnessed so many family meals, arguments, debates, and laughter. Nellie couldn't bear the vacant chair, the emptiness at her father's place.

"Why didn't we think to send him home to Ireland?" she questioned, plaintively. "Father asked so very little, but we all knew he was under Ireland's spell. Not any of us thought to subscribe to an Irish newspaper or take an Irish magazine. Something so simple, yet it would have given him such joy."

"Hush, Nellie. It's too late now," said Lizzie, patting her sister on the shoulder.

Nellie shook her off. "But why couldn't we have thought a little more about his pleasures?"

"Your father lived a good, long life," said ever-practical Letitia. "He worked hard and has reached his reward. Why would you think of Ireland, child, when your father has passed to Paradise?"

Nellie was silent. She had no answer, and while she firmly believed her father was embraced by a loving God, she couldn't shake the feeling a little pleasure on earth wasn't such a bad thing.

Late on a cold mid-winter afternoon, back on the farm her father and brothers had built from raw prairie, Nellie determined she would work towards making life in this world a little easier for people. The next world, the place that now housed her father's spirit, could wait. Nellie would focus her energies on the here and now. In the darkening kitchen, surrounded by familiar smells and warmed by tea and honey, Nellie Mooney resolved to carry on her work for social change.

# 5

## For Love or Money

*"I feel like I'm killing off some essential part
of myself, the part of me that dreams of great-
ness and fame. It is in writing that I can sway
the minds and hearts of many, and I am
about to slay that dream." – NLM*

Following the death of her father, Nellie decided
the best way to upgrade her own teaching licence
was to study at the Winnipeg Collegiate in order to
obtain a first-class teaching certificate.

Through the spring and fall of 1893 Nellie worked
and studied in Manitou. A coveted scholarship won her
six months' further education in Winnipeg. Her

Mr. and Mrs. Robert Wesley McClung. Despite early agonizing
over whether to marry, Nellie later claimed "cutting Wes
out of the herd" was the best thing she ever did.

months in the city, from December 1893 until August 1894, provided Nellie a wonderful opportunity to re-establish contact with her sister Hannah, already teaching in Winnipeg. The two boarded together and their close bonds tightened. Hannah knew the pressures of the first-class examinations; she had come first in the province the year before. Nellie's competitive spirit flared at the mention of her sister's triumph. She would do as well, or better, than Hannah.

And she did. As Hannah made plans to wed Baptist minister H.C. Sweet, "to leave the working world at last, settle down and have children," Nellie gained the highest educational qualifications possible. And, as though preordained, a job for Nellie came up in Treherne, sixty-eight kilometres north of Manitou. The same glorious September the Treherne schoolhouse got a new teacher, the local church was adjusting to their new minister. In August, just a month before Nellie was hired, the McClung family had moved from Manitou to Treherne to take the new posting. Nellie could continue to board with her chosen people, grow under the political and social tutelage of Mrs. McClung, and spend as much time as humanly possible with Wes.

∞

"I know I love him, Hannah, and I know I can be happy with Wes. We don't always agree but he's a fair fighter, and I know I would rather fight with him than agree with anyone else."

"Then what is it? You've been writing each other for months. He'll be back and forth between Treherne and Manitou all the time. His family is there and soon you'll be there. What's stopping you from setting a wedding date?"

Slowly packing her trunk for the move to Treherne, Nellie knew all too well what was stopping her. With Wes McClung she talked about matters close to her soul. They debated the nature of God, the matter of good and evil, eternal punishment, free will, and the doctrines of the Methodist and Presbyterian churches. Education, social issues, political reform; all things were dissected, discussed, and reassembled to be acceptable to the courting pair. But what Nellie hadn't mentioned to Wes was her conviction that entering into a union with him would destroy her hope of becoming a writer. Marriage was the death of creativity. Marriage meant the walls of a house closing in, endless labour, satisfying not one's own desire but the demands of a husband. Whose career would suffer? Hers, as a fledgling writer? Or his, as a businessman and pharmacist?

The words of Bellamy, an author Mr. Schultz had introduced, echoed in her ears:

> Wives should be in no way dependent on their husbands for maintenance. It is robbery as well as cruelty when men seize for themselves the whole product of the world and leave women to beg and wheedle for their share.

∞

Like Nellie, Wes moved out on his own. His parents and younger sister, also named Nellie, moved to

Treherne while he stayed in Manitou to manage the two drugstores he would eventually buy. With his pharmacology degree and the backing of his father, Wes seemed well set up for business. Very sports minded, he was an active participant in hockey, curling, and cycling clubs. In 1894, Wes McClung was also considered one of Manitou's most eligible bachelors. But his heart was set on Nellie Mooney, the firecracker thinker who lived in the midst of his family, many dusty prairie miles away.

∽

The crickets cheeped in the gently billowing fields as the stars seemed to multiply in the darkening summer sky. Nellie and Wes walked on, neither wanting the day to end nor the harmony of their time together to be disrupted by others. Near the parsonage, he spoke.

"You need not lay aside your ambitions for me, Nellie. I don't expect you to devote your whole life to me, but I do want you to know that you call out the very best in me."

"Do you think this is what they call love, Wes?"

"I do."

"Yes, I do, too," replied Nellie, "but if either of us found there was something beyond this, we mustn't hesitate to tell the other. And there would be no scenes, no recriminations: and we could go on liking each other always. Do you agree, Wes?"

He laughed then. "Of course I agree. I am very agreeable. I'm going back to Manitou tomorrow and I will send you something for your birthday that proves

exactly how much I agree." He suddenly became serious. "Nellie, I love the way you are, and what you do,
and your passion for people and words. I would not
want you to change."

∽

During harvest week, 1895, two years after her father's
death, a visit home showed Nellie where she was
needed. Instead of returning to the classroom, she
elected to stay home to help her mother.

For the third week the great kitchen was a hot-
house. Day and night the ovens were fired for baking
bread and making pies. There was ceaseless washing
up to do, and as soon as the kitchen was spotless the
work began again. Letitia never quit. How could
Nellie? She cooked and delivered huge meals to the
men working the fields. William and George banded
together to help Letitia. Then, their own crops had to
come off. The harvest had to be completed while
weather conditions were right, and the men needed
fuel, the small comfort of home-made food, in order to
carry on their race against dropping temperatures.

Still, the mundane tasks gave Nellie a chance to
think about her future and the red-haired young man
who had sent her an opal ring. Wes McClung's inten-
tions were clear. He planned to come to the farm as
soon as he could to meet her family. Both knew the
time had come to make a decision. So, why did Nellie
feel so awful? If she married Wes would *this* become
her life? Cooking, cleaning, baking, washing, and what
about babies? Little red-haired babies sprang up easily

in Nellie's imagination, but what about her as yet unwritten books? What about her dream of becoming an author and supporting herself and not being dependent on a husband? How could the two dreams coexist?

∞

After Christmas Nellie took a post at Northfield School, the place she had started her studies more than a decade before. How strange to stoke the same potbellied stove Mr. Schultz once fed kindling to on the coldest days of winter. How strange to see the same small desk where she once sat. But Nellie was deeply satisfied to see students, hungry to learn, burst through the schoolhouse door, and to walk home in the evening to Letitia and the unchanged landscape of her childhood.

Wes came for his planned visit in January of 1896. With the help of her mother, Nellie prepared a room. As she smoothed the worn quilt over the bed and fluffed the goose down pillow, a thought niggled. Jack, William, and George were plain country folk who spoke their mind and ate in the kitchen in their shirtsleeves. And Letitia. Would Wes be able to see beyond the bluntness to the fearless, undaunted woman who lived by the simple virtues industry and kindness to others? Would there be condescension in his tone? A surge of great protectiveness rose in Nellie. These were her people. They made her proud. She would stand or fall by these people.

"He's here!"

The shout went up from her mother, and Nellie raced to the window. Her heart surged. Wes McClung looked very handsome in a rough brown tweed suit. How could she have doubted him? Letitia took to Wesley like a mouse to cheese and, watching her mother and her future husband chat together by the fire, Nellie knew one of the important pieces of life's puzzle was in place.

On August 25, 1896, under grey, brooding skies, the Mooney-McClung wedding took place at the Millford Presbyterian church because the Methodist church couldn't hold the masses of people who came to wish the young couple well. Just before the ceremony, as Nellie adjusted her dress in the anteroom of the church, Letitia spoke.

"You've chosen well, Nellie," she said. "You've more sense than I've given you credit for. I like your young man. I couldn't have picked out a finer one myself. Wes will make a good husband, and you, despite your unconventional ways, will make him a fine wife."

This was the closest Letitia ever came to telling her daughter she loved her, and Nellie squeezed her mother's hand. Old hurts and rebellions faded as Nellie walked down the central aisle to join her groom at the front of the church.

Later, Wesley and Nellie McClung, married a scant two hours and ten minutes, clambered aboard a westbound train. After a brief honeymoon they were to return to the small, four-room flat above the Manitou drugstore. They'd bought furniture on an installment plan. Wes owned a two-thousand-dollar life insurance policy. Nellie would write her first novel. Flushed and excited with the prospect of travel and a new future as a married woman, Nellie felt hilariously, unreasonably happy. The century was soon to turn. A new era was dawning. She and Wes would face it together.

∞

"I refuse to consider it a waste, Wes. I've learned so much and it allowed me to sit in the kitchens of homes in Manitou I would never have been in before."

"But the magazine doesn't exist. The money is gone."

"That's true. The money is gone and *Town and Country* too good to be true," said Nellie, sighing. "It seems I won't do for Manitou what Dickens did for London, but I refuse to call it a waste of time. The stories I've heard and the things I've learned shall be stored up, for another assignment."

Nellie had been duped. Days before, she had been approached by a slick young salesman to write an article on Manitou for the inaugural issue of a new magazine. She handed over five dollars for a subscription and diligently set to researching her piece. The salesman, her money, and the magazine faded like a prairie rose.

Nellie's next encounter with a salesman won Wes's approval. She purchased a three-dollar cookbook entitled *Breakfast, Dinner and Supper* and decided to apply herself to the domestic arts. "Wes has cast his ballot in favour of the purchase," she noted, adding as a postscript. "I thought him a bit too enthusiastic."

⚭

Mere weeks into the marriage, Nellie felt an uneasy queasiness. Nine months later, on June 16, 1897, John Wesley McClung was born. "But I shall call him Jack," said Nellie, to her mother-in-law. "He came with a cry of distress but soon quieted when he found he was among friends." In naming her firstborn, Nellie paid tribute to her own brother, despite their lifetime quarrel. More babies came, in quick succession. By 1901 Florence and Paul had joined the McClung brood. Three children under the age of four kept Nellie busy.

At the mirror one morning she plucked a strand of grey hair from her head. Nellie was now twenty-eight years old. She had not written the books to make her famous. The mountainous washing pile shouted, and the children clamoured for food: "You can imagine my frame of mind," Nellie wrote, adding wryly, "In fact, the frame is all that is left of my mind."

⚭

What saved Nellie from home drudgery was the Women's Christian Temperance Union, the most progressive organization of its day. Women who wore the white ribbon of the Temperance Union were considered radical feminists. Unlike Ladies Aid organizations of various churches, the WCTU overrode denominational lines. In a circle where a woman was encouraged to speak her mind, where social and moral reform was a primary objective, Nellie felt at home. Women of Manitou banded together to make life better for their children. Roadhouses and pubs, cigarette stands, pool halls, and the daily glass of beer that stole from a child's well being came under fire. Equal franchise for both genders was part of the organization's mandate, as was training and funding orators and reciters. Nellie got her first taste of public speaking at a WCTU convention in Manitou in 1907. Once tasted, never without.

∞

Nellie was nervous when she first walked out on the stage in front of the crowd as a delegate to the convention. But, as they had always done in the past, written words saved her. Nellie looked down to her notes and began to read, slowly at first, until she forgot the audience and allowed herself to become lost in her powerful message of temperance and deliverance. Eyes misted, faces brightened, people understood. The air crackled with energy from the words she spoke, words she had laboured over for so long. Now, speech accomplished, standing in the wings, light-headed and basking in wave after wave of applause, Nellie knew what she was born for. Now she knew the heady power of a public address. The liquor traffic would be defeated and she, Nellie McClung, would be the one to continually trumpet the message. Still, the clapping continued.

∞

Three years after the birth of Horace, the McClungs' last planned child, E. Cora Hind arrived in Manitou.

Hind was a journalist with the *Winnipeg Free Press*, a woman who wrote for a living, and thus, an instant heroine to Nellie. While Nellie was teaching at Hazel School more than a decade earlier, the two women had met and taken an instant liking to each other. A correspondence grew between them, and on this sparkling fresh autumn day in 1909, Hind had arrived for an eight-day visit.

With a journalist's practised eye for detail, Hind watched Nellie negotiate extraordinary demands on her time and energy, noting twenty interruptions in a single morning after she'd engineered a reading in exchange for darning the family's socks.

"They all need something from you, don't they?" she commented, somewhat exasperated, after a neighbour woman asked Nellie to chair an ad hoc meeting.

"I've had a happy time all along," explained Nellie, cheerfully. "And I don't mind sharing it. The greatest thing in the world is to be a good neighbour."

Recalling the visit in an article entitled "Our Lady of Manitou" published in the *Ladies Home Journal* later that year, Hind wrote of Nellie: "She has, in a pre-eminent degree, that rare virtue, forgetfulness of self and the power to enter the lives and interest of others."

Hind's visit was life affirming for Nellie. The journalist respected Nellie's writing and encouraged her to seek a wider audience for the stories she crafted and cultivated behind closed doors. But the plunge had already been taken.

*Sowing Seeds in Danny*, Nellie's first novel, had been accepted by William Briggs Publishing Company the year before. The novel, published in 1908, would be read all across Canada and would eventually become a best-seller. It was a book about Western Canada, about the people Nellie had encountered in the parlours and kitchens of Manitou, when that fateful salesman had bilked her out of her five-dollar subscription.

Nellie passed her copy of *Sowing Seeds in Danny* over to Cora. "My mother-in-law challenged me to write a few years ago," she explained while Cora traced her dear friend's name embossed on the cover of the novel. "Colliers had a contest, and when I claimed I didn't have time to write – there was a church tea and Florence needed a new dress – she dismissed my excuses as trifles. She said life was conspiring to keep me tangled, and you know, Cora, she gave me the day, a whole day, to write."

Cora looked up from the pages. "And that resulted in this book?"

Nellie nodded. "Something else, Cora," she said, by this time grinning broadly. "I've been invited to read aloud. Yes, without interruption, at the WCTU Home for Friendless Girls in Winnipeg. I'm going to do it Cora, though I'm afraid no one will come. I've bought a new dress." Nellie pulled open a closet and showed her friend a cornflower blue dress.

"An elocutionist. How wonderful. You'll read from your book?"

"Yes, but I'll speak of other things too."

Cora beamed. "I have no doubt you will, Nellie. I have no doubt you will."

*Sowing Seeds in Danny*, Nellie's first novel, becomes a Canadian bestseller. Her "research" for the book was done by keeping an ear fine-tuned to the ways of the local rural people she loved.

| Friday, | WATERLOO PRESBYTERIAN CHURCH | Tickets |
|---|---|---|
| **Dec.** | **NELLIE L. McCLUNG,**<br>The popular Manitoban Novelist,<br>— Author of —<br>"Sowing Seeds in Danny" and "The Second Chance,"<br>In her Delightful Programme of | A Limited<br>Number |
| **16.** | | |
| at | **Readings and Recitations.**<br>Vocal and Instrumental Selections<br>by Leading Amateurs. | at<br>**25** |
| **8 p. m.** | "THE MAPLE LEAF FOREVER" | Cents. |

As a rising star in public speaking, Nellie is quick to introduce audiences to the political issues close to her heart.

# 6

## *Temperance and Equality*

*"The abduction of a young girl is punishable by five years' imprisonment but the stealing of a cow is punished by a fourteen-year sentence. Property has ever been held dearer than flesh and blood when the flesh and blood are woman's." – NLM*

A note, written in fourteen-year-old Jack's hand, sat beside Wes's dinner plate, but it was Nellie who saw it tucked between the saucer and the table napkin. Her husband and son had argued the night before about a misplaced hammer, and Jack's antidote was doggerel verse, a letter to his dad, explaining away the misunderstanding.

Good old Wes would worry less
If he were free from the store's distress

The childish scrawl bearing such truth prompted a rapid change in the McClung household. "I'd rather we live on less than see you drift into a state of nervous exhaustion," Nellie told her husband in the spring of 1911. Remembering her own childish worries about latching the henhouse door, Nellie knew Wes was afflicted with something she called the "primitive Methodist conscience," and was staying up late worrying about the possibility of incorrectly filled prescriptions. In a letter to a friend she wrote she refused to see Wes's "fresh complexion daily dulled by drugstore bleach."

Action was required. Nellie convinced Wes to sell the Manitou drugstores and to work as a handyman around two farms, which they bought (and subsequently rented to farmers) with the proceeds from the drug business. Requests for speaking engagements were constantly coming in, some addressed to "Canada's greatest entertainer and oratoress," and Nellie felt the family would better thrive with two happy parents. Wes agreed, but soon he brought something to the Manitou kitchen table to change the course of Nellie's life ever after.

∞

"It's a good opportunity for me, and it's only a hundred miles away, Nell."

"Yes, but Winnipeg? We've such a good life here, Wes. I've such stake in my small-town roots. Danny is all about small-town life "

"One of the agents with Manufacturers' will help us find a house in a good neighbourhood. Winnipeg is a city with over 136,000 people. It's booming. Half the population has come in the last six years and every one of them needs life insurance."

As the fire burned down in the front room fireplace, Nellie stared into its depths. She was thinking of something Letitia had told her years earlier. She'd said the happiest years a mother had were when her children were small, when she knew they were safe in their beds at night and, on her evening rounds, could listen to their gentle breathing. Nellie didn't believe it then, but now, on the cusp of change, she knew it to be true. During the day the Manitou house throbbed with laughter and life; at night it basked in a gentle slumber. Now those days were drawing to a close. For fifteen years, not including her time as a young teacher, she'd lived in Manitou.

Wes broke into her meditation.

"We'll buy or rent a cottage on Lake Winnipeg for the summer until we find our new house. What do you think?"

Nellie's smile was wan. "I think it will be an adventure for the children, for all of us, but I shall miss the busy, easy sociability of this special place."

"Yes," said Wes, cupping his wife's cheek and drawing her towards him. "We all will."

∞

By August 5, 1911, Manitou and Nellie's eldest son Jack, who had stayed to write his entrance examinations for Wesley College, were a sweet memory. The summer at Matlock Beach with the three younger children had fled, and the rambling house at 97 Chestnut Street, Winnipeg, with a special room to write, was Nellie's new reality. Between that and the sure evidence that a fifth McClung child was on the way, the empty rooms in the new house would soon fill up.

The birth of Mark McClung in October of 1911 barely slowed Nellie. In typical fashion she was gathering an ever-growing circle of friends. Cora Hind, delighted to have Nellie in the city, invited her to the Canadian Women's Press Club, and there, with militant suffragists from Britain and Ontario, the Winnipeg faction schemed for the voting rights of women.

Emmeline Pankhurst, visiting reformer from Britain, alerted Nellie and her colleagues to the plight of the "foreigner," the non-Anglo-Saxon female worker in Winnipeg's small factories.

"It's not enough for us to meet in the comforts of this club, talking and eating chicken sandwiches and olives," chided Pankhurst. "We must organize. We must sway public sentiment in favour of those who are not here. Many, many, women in this city are working long hours for small wages under appalling working conditions."

Pankhurst was right. The north end of Winnipeg was alive with Eastern European immigrants recruited by Ottawa to take land in western Canada. Many had ventured only as far as Winnipeg and were left to survive – or not – in a new and cruel winter climate. Unlike Nellie's homogeneous Manitou, Winnipeg's poor, especially the newly landed immigrant working-poor, were very evident and in no short supply. As a result of the huge influx of people, hasty tenement housing had sprung up. Landlords got rich as rapidly as their housing turned to slums. Like the raw sewage that spawned them, typhoid and smallpox ran unchecked through the communities.

The local Council of Women decided a female factory inspector was needed if the lives of Winnipeg women were to improve. Nellie and a woman named Mrs. Claude Nash were recruited to visit Manitoba's premier, arch-Conservative Sir Rodmond Roblin. Their mission was to take him to the least savoury side of the city and expose him to Pankhurst's harsh realities.

The drama of social reforms brought to the high stages of the legislature was a potent draw for Nellie She felt empowered by her peers and ready to confront Premier Roblin with the plight of the city's poor.

A large, slightly florid, good-looking man in his early sixties rose as the women entered the room. Sir Rodmond had an eye for a fine figure, and the two young women, fresh-faced and comely in hats and gloves, were a pleasant change from the dull bureaucrats who peopled his day. Except for a ten-year Liberal rule under Thomas Greenway, the political machine – wrought of patronage and power – had seen a Tory at the helm since Manitoba's inception. Roblin felt genial and unthreatened by the two pretty young reformers who wanted him to accompany them on a factory tour. An afternoon with the lovely

Mrs. Nash and the newly arrived and formidable Mrs. McClung might be just the break he needed from political duty.

"Hard work is good for young people," he assured the women as his driver took the car down narrowing streets pointing to the city's north end. Resting his plump hand on the gold head of his cane, Roblin waxed philosophical, musing about his own wholesome country youth. "There's too much idleness now, with electricity and shortcuts in labour. Why, as a boy, I myself worked from sunup until sundown, and it was hard work that got me to where I am today."

The women, on either side, exchanged glances. Nellie's eyes widened momentarily but Roblin didn't notice. "These young girls are working because they want pin money. They're likely living at home, and in fact," he wagged a fat finger first at Nellie and then her companion, "I don't think they should be taking these jobs away from men."

As the car moved through shabby streets, Roblin glanced out the passenger window. Frowning at the grime, he changed his tone and took a stab at the multitude of foreigners – some shiftless bohunks – who certainly had found better lives in Canada. "What do they expect?" he asked. "Flower beds of ease? It doesn't do women any harm to learn how money comes. Extravagant women are the curse of this age."

Nellie bade the driver stop in front of a factory. A dank stairwell descended into an airless basement room. Roblin, clutching his cane and looking decidedly uncomfortable, manoeuvred carefully around the slush and trash littering his approach.

Inside the basement room, he clutched his buffalo robe. There was no ventilation and no heat. The suffocating dim room, lit by bare light bulbs, was heated by human bodies in close quarters. Scores of women were hunched over sewing machines that droned on incessantly despite the intrusion of strangers. The floors of the factory were littered with discarded scraps of cloth and bits of food.

Rodmond turned to the nearest worker, a woman who had been briefly alerted to their presence by the blast of fresh air that marked their arrival. "Doesn't anyone clean the floors in here?" Roblin shouted over the rattle of her sewing machine. The woman shook her head mutely, shrugged, and continued running a thick bolt of cut cloth through the machine.

"She can't really talk," explained Mrs. Nash gently. "English is likely not her first language, and moreover, these women are paid by the piece. They labour from 8:00 in the morning until 6:00 in the evening. The less time they take away from their machines, the more they get paid. I don't expect anyone will want to engage us in conversation."

As though on cue, one woman rose from her station to scamper down a dark passageway. The foul stench wafting from an opened door was testimony of inadequate plumbing and lack of sanitation in the toilets. Roblin clutched his linen handkerchief to his face and made blindly for the door, his eyes awash. "I can't bear this," he cried, as he heaved his bulk up the stairwell.

At street level, the premier gained some composure. "Yes, yes, well, that was indeed distasteful. I shall have my factory inspector look into that brutal mess, but for the time being, ladies, I'm afraid you'll have to excuse me. I have forgotten an important business engagement."

"Your factory inspector *has* been notified of this and many other sweatshops," said Nellie. "The garment industry is terribly exploitive. You've seen for yourself, Sir Rodmond. We want a female factory inspector appointed who has training in social work. We want a woman who will do something to improve these terrible conditions."

Sir Rodmond Roblin drew himself up, his face fired with indignation. "I have too much respect for women to even consider giving one a job like that. That place is a hellhole, not at all fit for a woman. I still don't understand why you two would ferret out such an utterly disgusting place. Trust me, Mrs. Nash, Mrs. McClung, I am greatly disturbed having witnessed that." He jabbed a plump finger towards the gloomy stairwell, "I will endeavour to speak to the proper authorities about it, but, for the time being, I have other matters to attend to. Come along, ladies."

∽

Reporting back to the local Council of Women, Nellie was horrified to discover the association would not support her current work. Most of the women seemed afraid to associate with controversy, and a large number reported their husbands strictly forbade "activities" associated with foreigners. Meddling women, the men declared, would threaten job security.

Fifteen women out of the larger organization agreed to establish a new association, the Political Equality League. Their mandate was to gather first-hand information on the status of women in Manitoba, and indeed the entire Dominion. Public speakers would alert the world to their findings in order to sway public opinion.

Leaning back on fellow activist Jane Hample's best needlepoint chair, Nellie McClung felt a physical rush through her body. The real work was just beginning. She instinctively rose to the challenge of enticing a crowd. Reading aloud from *Sowing Seeds in Danny* was a wonderful experience, but, this – this was far more important.

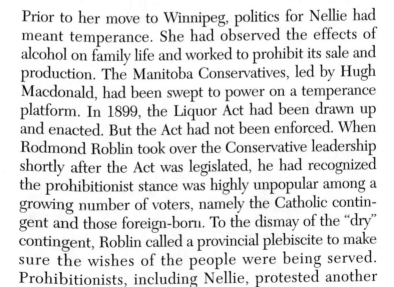

Prior to her move to Winnipeg, politics for Nellie had meant temperance. She had observed the effects of alcohol on family life and worked to prohibit its sale and production. The Manitoba Conservatives, led by Hugh Macdonald, had been swept to power on a temperance platform. In 1899, the Liquor Act had been drawn up and enacted. But the Act had not been enforced. When Rodmond Roblin took over the Conservative leadership shortly after the Act was legislated, he had recognized the prohibitionist stance was highly unpopular among a growing number of voters, namely the Catholic contingent and those foreign-born. To the dismay of the "dry" contingent, Roblin called a provincial plebiscite to make sure the wishes of the people were being served. Prohibitionists, including Nellie, protested another enumeration. Previous referendums had instituted the law, and so the law should stand. The prohibitionists' decision to boycott the count backfired, however. The plebiscite was pushed through, and with prohibitionists under-represented, Roblin's government was able to repeal Macdonald's Liquor Act, and call it "the choice of the people."

A man unwilling to totally alienate anyone, Roblin had agreed individual municipalities could petition government for Prohibition if they could demonstrate a majority of ratepayers agreed temperance was best in their community. In Manitou, Nellie and her fellow prohibitionists had taken countless petitions to cabinet. Each had been dismissed as flawed, even though the desire for a dry community was clearly indicated on the petitions.

Now that she lived in Winnipeg and knew the great premier personally, Nellie's political education was evolving. While temperance was still on her agenda, women's rights became her rallying cry. More than half of Manitoba's population had no legal status, Dower rights, well established in Ontario, were nonexistent in the booming West. Without consultation, a man could sell the family home, collect all the money, and abandon his wife and children on the roadside while he left to seek better prospects elsewhere. The inheritance of land went exclusively to sons, regardless of a daughter's contribution, and in some cases, mothers did not even have legal rights to their own offspring. It made Nellie's blood boil.

Ring. Ring. Ring. The telephone at 95 Chestnut Street, September 1912:

"Mrs. McClung? This is Mrs. Kay Redson calling. We'd be so honoured if you would accept our invitation to the Portage la Prairie Anglican Ladies Aid next month for a recitation from your wonderful book."

And ever-affable Nellie's response: "Thank-you. Yes, I'd be delighted. I wonder if I might be allowed to discuss the current political situation following the recital. Is that something your guests might agree to Mrs. Redson?... "

∽

Women's suffrage was not a popular topic in the early part of the last century. Women suffragists were called "suffragettes," originally a disparaging term first used by a London newspaper, but adopted for themselves by British women activists. When the Women's Political Equality League set up a booth to distribute literature at the Winnipeg Stampede in 1912, they were met with derision.

Whisper campaigns claimed suffragettes were short-haired women consorting with long-haired men. Many ill-informed people believed suffragettes wanted total role reversal and were dissatisfied with their gender. Home and family were at stake, and the idea that a woman could be both a mother, a wife, *and* a voting member of society was a hard sell.

In many ways, Nellie quelled those dismissive impulses. With her plain-speaking friendliness and her penchant towards fashion, family, and the winsome ways of a good hat, Nellie reminded people that femininity and politics were not mutually exclusive.

"The women's movement, which has been scoffed at and jeered at and misunderstood, most of all by the people it is destined to help, is a spiritual revival of the best instincts of womanhood – the instinct to serve and save the race," she wrote.

∞

The room was hushed. Nellie gripped the lecturn and looked into the upturned faces of good, law-abiding Christian women. She didn't miss the fact that not a face among them stood out. Grey hair competed with blond and brunette, but the skin colour of the entire audience was uniform. Still, these good white women needed to know the truth. Nellie took a breath and launched into her speech using language they would understand, the parable of the Prodigal Son.

"The road from Jerusalem to Jericho is the world today, here and now, and there are operating on the road as deadly, cowardly and merciless thieves as ever beat and robbed a defenceless traveler. Eighty thousand young girls are trapped every year into a life of shame, some of them as sweet and pure and innocent as your daughters and mine."

Nellie could detect the inhalation of breath. She continued.

"Hundreds and thousands of young girls and women are employed in sweated industries, where a living wage is not paid them, while rich men grow richer as a result of unpaid toil. One boy out of every fifth family becomes a drunkard to support the legalized liquor traffic. Have you a boy to spare to keep up the revenue?" Nellie's rhetoric was met by silence.

"Men and women were intended to work together and will work more ideally than apart, and just as the mother's influence as well as the father's is needed in the bringing up of children and in the affairs of the home, so are they needed in the larger home, the state. Men alone cannot make just laws for men and women, just as any class of people cannot legislate justly for another class."

A woman in the middle of the audience near the aisle stood and pointedly walked from the room. More chairs scraped the floor as people stood to leave. But they weren't all leaving. Many leaned forward, hanging on Nellie's words.

"A great many women have not known that the law discriminates against women. Now they are finding it out and voicing their indignation. To make laws regarding women more stringent is offensive to some men, and these men are voters, and the women who seek for these changes are not voters."

The room swirled, the faces ran together. Nellie pressed on, speaking to the ceiling, to the air, to the hope within herself:

"But the day is breaking and the darkness is fleeing away. Four million women in the United States now enjoy full parliamentary franchise. Women vote in New Zealand, Australia, Iceland, and Finland and have some measure of franchise in many other countries…"

The clapping overwhelmed her last worlds. The room was alive with it, electrified. The suffrage movement, with Nellie on the podium, was steadily adding more women to its ranks.

The suffragists, with young Mark McClung in their midst, gain momentum
from the visit of British feminist and activist Emmeline Pankhurst to Edmonton in 1916.

# 7

## Of Votes and Roasts

*"I feel that when a man offers hat-lifting when we ask for justice we should tell him to keep his hat right on. I will go further and say that we should tell him not only to keep his hat on but to pull it right down over his face." – NLM*

The women huddled, bound together by disappointment tempered with a certain unmistakable air of excitement. The Political Equality League had just come from the 1914 winter sitting of the Manitoba legislature where, as expected, their first formal request for voting rights for women had been flatly turned

down. Nellie bowed out of the League's hastily con-
vened post-mortem at the home of Lillian Thomas. The
meeting with Roblin had resulted in its predictable out-
come, and other matters played on her mind.

Young Mark, not yet three years old, had been up
half the night with a hacking cough. Nellie knew
Lillian, a particularly close journalist chum from the
Press Club, was hatching a very public rebuttal to
Roblin's vapid declaration that giving women the right
to vote would ruin many a good home. It was incredi-
ble how he clung to the old stereotypes. But as much
as she longed to participate in a pithy retort to set the
premier back a step or two, Nellie needed to see to her
own house. While the other activists gathered to exe-
cute their defence scheme, she hurried home under
leaden February skies to check on Mark.

Their champion wasn't far from her friends'
thoughts, however. "We'll ask Nellie to play Roblin.
She's the only one who can mimic that voice," said
Lillian, after floating the idea of a satirical burlesque
show. Puffing up her cheeks and screwing up her face,
Lillian attempted to repeat the premier's scathing
words. *"To project a woman into the sphere of party
politics would be to cause her to desert her true sphere,
that of the hearth and home, and abandon her children
to servant girls, a grave danger to all society."*

The women laughed. "That's not bad, Lillian. Are
you sure you shouldn't play Roblin yourself?"

Thomas shook her head. "No. I'll book the Walker
Theatre and do all the advertising. To do this mock
parliament justice, I think we need Nellie McClung in
our starring role. Nobody could play Sir Rodmond the

way she can. Nell knows that fine, old-school gentleman well and she's not afraid to take the mickey out of anyone, regardless of rank."

∞

The house was packed. A buzz persisted even after the house lights dimmed and the curtain rose to reveal female legislators cloaked in black choir robes over evening gowns. A few anticipatory snickers could be heard from the audience, and as the petitions were brought forward and read, the few snickers turned to outright belly laughs. Decent men should not be seen about town wearing scarlet ties or squeaky shoes. Six-inch collars should be banned in public. Labour-saving devices should be provided for the worn down and weary male. The crowd roared approval. A final petition suggested alkali should be banned by manufacturers of laundry soap, as it ruined men's delicate hands.

Gaiety doubled when Mr. R.C. Skinner took to the boards and requested an audience with the premier. He pushed a wheelbarrow full of petitions, all requesting votes for men. Nellie, dressed as her nemesis Sir Rodmond, roared to centre stage, cloaks flowing. What she lacked of the premier in appearance, she made up in gesture, manner, and tone. With searing sarcasm and just the right tinge of irony, she congratulated Mr. Skinner on his appearance.

"I wonder about interfering with a civilization that can produce a splendid figure of manhood such as yourself, Mr. Skinner," she crooned, shaking her head in mock approval. "Oh no, I believe man is made for something higher and better than voting. Men are made to support families. What is a home without a bank account?"

Nellie turned to the crowd. "Politics unsettles men, and unsettled men means unsettled bills, broken furniture, and broken vows, and divorce!" Lowering her tone from booming condescension to patronizing sentiment, Nellie wagged her head back and forth. "When you ask for the vote for men, you are asking me to break up peaceful, happy homes, to wreck innocent lives, and this is something I will not do."

Thunderous applause broke out, and a fellow Political Equality League member bearing a bouquet of roses for Nellie rushed across the stage. "They're from the Manitoba Liberal party, the loyal Opposition," she whispered mischievously as she handed Nellie the flowers. "A token of appreciation for the female premier's eloquence."

∞

The women's burlesque was a riotous whirl, but it was underpinned with a serious message. So, too, the flowers. While not officially from the Liberal party but rather from two audience members with decidedly Liberal leanings, the intent was unmistakable. Two months later, Nellie and a colleague were invited to give an address on female suffrage at the Liberal convention in downtown Winnipeg. An election was to be held in June, and the issue was clear: the Conservatives would not support giving women a vote, but the Liberals would, if they got elected. Nellie, with her eye firmly on the goal of female suffrage, began an intensive cross-province tour campaigning for the Liberal party.

∞

"Her husband must be dead."

"No, he's alive."

"An alcoholic?"

"Not that I've heard. But I have heard he's thinking of divorce."

"Who could blame him." Pause. "Do they have little ones?"

"Aye, a huge brood. I've heard eight or nine, all close in age with the youngest still an infant."

"And who looks after the children while she's out and about gallywagging?"

"I don't know. I think the children run wild in the streets, totally unsupervised."

"Poor wee things. Not a one of them asked to be born a McClung. How terribly sad."

∞

Nellie was far from immune to criticism, but the most painful and the most internalized was when the media targeted her children. Mark was only three years old when she did most of her travelling. Horace was eight and Paul was thirteen, just finishing grade school. The elder two, Jack and Florence, were seventeen and fifteen, and well accustomed to their mother's absence. They read about Nellie's adventures in Brandon,

Neepawa, Minnedosa, Dauphin and every whistle stop in between. Accounts would be trumpeted or blasted in the press, depending on the editor's political alliance.

Even the younger children quickly became used to their mother being constantly in the public spotlight.

Horace, rescuing a very spattered young Mark from a muddy wrestling match with a neighbour boy, took the bedraggled youngster down the back lane and put him into the yard through a concealed passage in the back fence. "We'll go see Dad," he consoled. "It's a good thing I got to you first before the *Telegraph* got a photograph of yet another of Nellie McClung's neglected children!"

∞

Despite the Liberals' best efforts, no amount of campaigning could wrest power away from the Conservatives. The July 10, 1914 election saw the defeat of Liberal leader T.C. Norris, whom many considered weak for his acceptance of female suffrage. His party did, however, take a huge chunk out of the Conservative majority. The Tory lead in the house dropped from sixteen to seven and the Liberals substantially won the popular vote.

Nellie, deeply disappointed in the results, convinced Wes to spend some time at their beach house following the election. Nellie's sister Lizzie rented a nearby cottage with her two teenage daughters and, as in days gone by, Nellie poured out her hopes, dreams, disappointments, and wild imaginings to Elizabeth, who shared her family history if not her vision for emancipated women.

"I've never felt such unity of purpose," Nellie confided as the weeks stretched into two months of blissful idleness. She was still talking of the election, holding the hand of her husband as they strolled down Matlock Beach. "Even though we didn't win, I feel as though we have united the women of Manitoba in a great cause."

Wes looked at Nellie. The wind had shaken her hair loose and the sun was setting behind her. She was soon to turn forty-one years old. The campaigning had taken its toll. But Wes did not see the lines in her forehead and the hint of crow's-feet at Nellie's eyes. Instead, he saw political fire undimmed, and merriment still playing in her eyes.

"You've done well, Nell," he said, fondly. He squinted into the sun's afterglow. "I wonder what is next." Nellie followed his gaze. The sky was pink, the air warm, and the lake still. The moment was magical, suspended in time. Nellie would often think back wistfully to that peaceful walk. The following day, August 4, 1914, Britain declared war on Germany.

∞

The McClung family stayed at the beach until August 24, but each day, as the train from the city came bearing husbands and fathers with newspapers tucked under their arms, the news of war worsened. The antics of Norris and Roblin in the House of Assembly were relegated to page three of the *Winnipeg Free*

*Press*. Britain was asking for allies. Troop trains were leaving the station weekly. The world, including Winnipeg, was at war.

The smaller children walked ahead, each carrying relics from their summer at the beach. Strolling behind the parade of children, Nellie admired their nut-brown bodies and their strength as, laden, they lugged baskets and hampers and bits and pieces of a joyous summer to the station. She imagined sand in their shoes and smiled, remembering the easy quality of their days. What would happen now?

Looking back at the shuttered cottage, Nellie shivered. "It looks forlorn," she said to Jack, who trudged along beside her. "It has the blinded look of a dead thing."

Jack, now taller than Nellie, redistributed his load to take his mother's arm. "You'll be back next summer and it will be the same as always." He paused and without knowing its import asked the question Nellie had prayed she would not hear. "Mother, when will I be old enough to join the army?"

# 8

## Sorrow of War, Joy of Action

*"War is a crime committed by men and, therefore, when enough people say it shall not be, it cannot be. This will not happen until women are allowed to say what they think of war." – NLM*

With a war raging, the women of Winnipeg took action to collect supplies for hospital ships. The Public Works department shut down, casting unenlisted men out of work. Unemployment grew steadily, and with it, drinking. As more and more demoralized men turned to the bottle for comfort, Nellie and her political allies struggled to bring temperance back to the floor.

New hats take the place of champagne as Nellie celebrates women's suffrage reaching Alberta in the spring of 1916. Together with Alice Jamieson (centre) and Emily Murphy (right), she poses for a formal portrait to commemorate the event.

Their march on the legislature to request the reopening of Public Works and a ban on the sale of intoxicants was met with a Conservative walkout in October. Roblin, as haughty as ever, told Opposition leader T. C. Norris Nellie's people were "friends of yours, not ours" and then commanded Tory members to leave the House.

For the Political Equality League and the nation in general, it was a discouraging time. Winter was coming, reminders of war were everywhere, and the heady times of last spring, when suffrage and women's rights seemed on everyone's lips, seemed mute and distant.

In mid-December 1914, Wes broke the mood. The insurance company had offered him a transfer to Edmonton or Vancouver and a new job as a branch manager. How did Nellie feel about leaving Winnipeg for adventures farther West?

Such a simple question, yet so complex. Nellie wasn't naive. She knew the Liberals were bound to take power in the next election. Rumours of scandal and misappropriation of funds from Ottawa plagued the Conservatives. Other rumours, that she would almost certainly be offered the first-ever female cabinet posting – the Honourable Mrs. Nellie McClung, Minister of Education – were flying as thick and fast as winter snows. But Wes, who stalwartly endorsed her every decision even when it meant her absence, now had an opportunity for himself.

Edmonton beckoned. Nellie's brother William and his family were there. Nellie smiled as she remembered Will's determination to find hope in a new land. She recalled his quick smile as he boarded the coach on Garafraxa Road so many years ago and left to seek his fortune. He, above the others, carried on, moved from the farm near Wawanesa farther West, as though conquest and new adventure were in his blood.

But so much had happened in Winnipeg. Here, Nellie had grown up. In Manitou, life had been about family. Here in Winnipeg, it was about the extended family, the human family, and particularly about giving voice to that family's silent sisterhood.

"We'll go to Edmonton, Wes," Nellie declared, one morning shortly after the subject was raised. "I will shed all my political alliances and go back to the work I like best. Writing."

Wes shook his head, happy and bemused. "I'll book us tickets on the Grand Trunk Pacific, Nell, but, as for shedding politics, it would be just as likely you make not a single friend in Edmonton."

∞

Making friends was something that came naturally to Nellie, and the fresh frontiers of Edmonton in 1915 provided a new staging ground for her dynamic personality. "The whole atmosphere of the city was young, hopeful and full of surprises," she reminisced more than twenty years later in her autobiography. "Expectancy was in the air. It may have been the high altitude which stimulated me, but I never felt better or more keenly alive."

Once again, as before, faithful friend E. Cora Hind descended to check out Nellie's new circumstances. What she found was Nellie associating with all and sundry, but particularly aligned with the Edmonton Equal Franchise League and the Canadian Women's Press Club and quarterbacking plans for a temperance campaign. Among the female power-brokers of her new domain, Nellie made acquaintance with the only female magistrate in the British Empire, Alice Jamieson, and her friend Emily Murphy, who would be appointed a magistrate the following year. Nellie with these two women proved a potent combination.

∞

"I've recently finished this, Cora," said Nellie, pushing a bundle of papers across the table to her friend. "It's different from *Danny* and my collection of Manitou stories. I'm a different woman now. Those four years in Winnipeg were politically charged and now, this. War. Both have changed me."

The two friends were sitting together in the makeshift sun porch of the McClungs' new home near the riverbank. The North Saskatchewan swam lazily in the distance, a serpentine glimpse of bluish green. "Yes," said Cora, "I know, but they have changed you for the better." Turning her attention to the manuscript, she glanced at the title. *"In Times Like These.* When in the world did you have time for this?"

"Moving here has given me time. And time has allowed me to distil my thoughts. This is the result." Nellie tapped the fat manuscript. "I'm unquiet about this war and my book attempts to explain. Both sides are wrong. It's not about the two sides, one good, the other evil. If there were women of power and authority in the German Reichstag, this war would not have started."

"I really believe that, Cora. The two are tied together as surely as you and I are lifelong friends. Listen. A delegation for women's suffrage is going to the Alberta legislature this fall and I plan to be a part of that campaign. But for the last few months I have been thinking long and hard about what the war means to Christians, and more specifically to Christian women." She smiled wryly at her friend. "The *Saturday Night* people read the manuscript. They called it "hysterical and fantastic bunkum.""

"In that case," said Cora, gathering the pages onto her lap. "I'm sure to love it."

∞

The war actually furthered Nellie's dual causes. The temperance movement employed the Direct Legislation Act of 1914 to force a plebiscite in Alberta. Seventy-five thousand copies of the Act were distributed across the province. If the majority voted dry, the government, under Liberal Premier A. L. Sifton, would be forced to ban the sale of "Old King Alcohol." Nellie was heavily involved, campaigning and speaking in town halls, church basements, and school auditoriums. Wherever she was invited, the call was the same: Vote temperance and improve the lives of women and children everywhere by eliminating the temptations of liquor.

∞

The day before the July 21, 1915 election, Nellie was feeling frustrated. As part of the Edmonton Equal Franchise League she had organized a parade down Jasper Avenue. Twelve hundred women thronged the pavement, and while many initially had thought the parade a good idea, out on the street, they felt exposed. Some were hedging. Was it not undignified to walk down the centre of a public thoroughfare?

Nellie felt her patience wearing thin. There were so many people. The sky was a relentless blue and it was a beautiful day to walk. Why would they hesitate now, when the mood was jubilant, the sun shining? A very old woman at Nellie's elbow seemed determined to speak. She had come to march. Where should she go? Nellie turned, noting the woman's withered leg and the crutch she held. "Would you mind taking others with you in your car?" asked Nellie.

"I haven't come to drive," responded the old woman, "I've come to march with the rest."

"But the course is three miles from start to finish."

"Your women are welcome to ride in my car, if they like, but I intend to walk."

Nellie peered more closely into the woman's tiny, bright eyes. Her face reminded Nellie of a leaf, frost-bitten time and time again, nearly winter-killed. How much was due to a man escaping into drink? How intolerably had she suffered? "Yes" said Nellie, lifting her chin and looking forward through the crowds, "Would you do me the honour of allowing me to walk beside you?"

The march began. Every time the crutch of Nellie's companion touched the pavement, the woman whispered three words in a rapid sequence. Nellie strained to hear. "Dry-dry-dry." Step. "Dry-dry-dry." Step. "Dry-dry-dry."

∞

In Edmonton alone, ninety-three polling booths were set up to take the count. The six women staffing each booth were jubilant and certain the "dry" contingent would triumph. By the evening of July 21, 1915, the votes were counted. Of fifty-five provincial ridings, thirteen voted wet. The rest, 58,295 votes, opted for a dry Alberta. The reformers won the day, showing a two to one majority in favour of Prohibition. The news felt like a sweet, sweet victory for a sunburned and exhausted Nellie McClung.

∞

Rest, that glorious summer, was not to be had. Three days after the Prohibition referendum an urgent telegram came from various leaders of the Manitoba Liberals. An election had been called two weeks hence. Two telegrams came with these appeals:

> Most essential that you give us your assistance. STOP. People are asking for you all over the country. STOP. Everyone clamouring for your appearance to top off campaign properly. STOP.

There was no hesitation. The Liberals guaranteed women's suffrage in Manitoba if elected. Nellie was on the train the next day. Like King Midas, Nellie McClung turned everything she touched into gold. She was beloved. She was sincere. She spoke from her heart. On August 7, 1915, hot on the heels of Alberta Prohibition, Manitoba elected a Liberal government ripe with the promise the Women's Suffrage Bill would be drafted to receive its first reading as soon as the House reconvened.

At home in Alberta, the writing was on the wall. Premier Sifton pledged to go beyond a discussion of women's suffrage in the legislature. He announced he would introduce the bill as a government measure. It was certain to pass.

Nellie took to the podium. Her words were triumphant. "Women's suffrage is arriving. We didn't have to knock anybody down and take it away from them. It is going to be handed to us with kindest regards and best wishes. We are so glad that we do not have to fight any more, we are tired of war, tired of campaigns and petitions and signatures and interviews!"

On the home front, social reforms were surging head, but news from the battlefields in Europe was bleaker and bleaker. And Nellie was now personally involved.

∽

"But I'm eighteen, now."

"And that means what? You're old enough to kill someone?"

"I want to go, Mother. I want to help the British Empire, while one still exists."

Nellie had known it was coming. How could she let Jack go into what she thought of as "the inferno of war?" And yet, knowing his call to arms came not in the intoxication of victory but when the Allies were at a low ebb, how could she hold him back without breaking his heart?"

She looked straight into the eyes of her eldest son. The blue was so like the blue of Wes's eyes, so filled with gentleness and love and pity for his fellow man. Her son had never held a gun, and yet she could tell what would soon transpire. Jack's childhood would be put away forever. He might become fodder for the ammunition makers, he might be left alone to die in the trenches, but he was willing to go, for he believed the cause was just. She saw it in his eyes.

"Go, Jackie boy," said Nellie, her heart breaking within. "I must believe it is right and that some good should come from this evil." She reached out to stroke his strawberry blond hair, but he was gone. With a whoop and a holler, Jack McClung sought his friends. He enlisted that very day.

Early on a cold and overcast morning, December 4, 1915, Jack hoisted his duffel bag up onto the train. He remained jovial, said goodbye to his family and friends, but choked with emotion in his father's embrace. "Oh Dad! Good old Dad!" was all Jack could muster. As Nellie walked home that morning she noticed the blinds still closed on a neighbouring home. They reminded her uncomfortably of the lining of a coffin. She later wrote: "When we came home I felt strangely tired and old though I am only forty-two. I know that my youth has departed from me. It has gone with Jack, our beloved, our firstborn, the pride of our hearts."

∽

On January 27, 1916, a third reading of the bill to enfranchise Manitoba women was read and passed by the Liberal government. Not only did the bill allow women the vote, it also enabled them to be elected to the legislature. In the House of Assembly the galleries overflowed with women waving the suffragist colours, purple and yellow. When it was finally announced that women were voters, a wild roar went up. The stands quieted momentarily and a lone voice, reed-thin and wavering in the echoing chamber, could be heard singing "O Canada." Other voices joined. Soon the House was filled with the sound of women singing in unison. Up and down the melody their voices trilled, strong and true. "Our home and native land." Ours. The voices sounded with pride and ownership. Never had these words felt so inclusive. It was an emotional and historic moment. And it was to be repeated in other provinces.

In Saskatchewan, women won the right to vote and run for provincial office on March 14. In Alberta, Premier Sifton followed the lead of Manitoba's Premier T.C. Norris, and in April the Alberta Charter was amended to allow all persons over the age of twenty-one, male and female, the right to vote and run for provincial office.

∽

They strolled, three abreast, down Jasper Avenue. On April 19, 1916, the day Alberta women succeeded in winning the right to vote, Nellie was with two women, both magistrates. Alice Jamieson from Calgary was visiting the capital to witness the historic reading with Nellie McClung and Emily Murphy, now a local magistrate. The three women were jubilant, their arms linked, as they strutted down the still-slushy street. They felt vibrant and energetic, as if a rare chinook wind had brought the promise of spring to a cold city.

"We should celebrate," said Alice. "If it weren't for your Prohibition laws, Nellie, I would shout you all a drink to mark the occasion."

Nellie laughed. "It does feel like we need to mark the day, doesn't it?"

Emily swung in front of the other two women and directed their gaze to a shop front. It was a milliner's, and in the window were seven beautiful hats.

"Let's buy ourselves hats," said Emily, eyes twinkling. Upon the startled shop girl the merry trio descended, ooohing and ahhhing at each other as they tried on the splendid hats adorned with feathers or flowers or filigree brocade. After each had settled on her own style and paid for the purchase, the women slipped outside to admire themselves yet again, in the store window.

"Now, we shall be photographed," said Nellie decisively, tapping the top of her wide-brimmed new hat. "After years and years of struggle, women in Alberta have won the right to vote and it shall never be reversed." She stuck out her elbows and both friends linked arms again. Off the three went, peacock proud, in search of a photography studio. Victory had come at last, and it was as sweet and fresh as the spring air.

# 9

## Equity and Elections

*"I believed that we [politicians] were the
executive of the people and should bring our
best judgement to bear on every question,
irrespective of party ties." – NLM*

As women's suffrage leapfrogged from province to
province, so Nellie's career as a public speaker
escalated. In early 1915 she was the keynote speaker
at a temperance rally in British Columbia, and in
October the same year she toured her birth province,
fuelled by the fact that Ontario had neither enfran-
chised women nor passed any legislation regarding the
sale of alcohol. Easterners loved her. The press

Nellie McClung, MLA.
She is elected to the Alberta legislature in 1921.

dubbed Nellie "bright, breezy, brimming with optimism."

One dark spot marred her Eastern tour. The Ontario Equal Franchise Association underestimated Nellie's drawing power and, in seeing the crowds, tried to decrease their agreed-upon payment for the lecture. An anonymous letter, leaked to the press, claimed Nellie demanded monies pegged for a patriotic fund, and the next morning's headlines blared, "Suffrage Meeting Scandal." Nothing could be further from the truth but Nellie felt humiliated by the experience, her reputation besmirched. "I lost something," she wrote in her journal. "I was never quite so sure of people after that... I grew sophisticated at last, but it came the hard way."

To the south, Americans welcomed Nellie warmly. In 1916 her lecture at the National American Women's Suffrage Association was so successful she was invited on a six-week, forty-city U.S. tour in the fall. Florence, now seventeen, travelled with her mother on this rail adventure that reaped two hundred dollars a week, plus expenses, as Nellie McClung spoke for the empowerment of women across the United States.

If not for the spectre of war casting its grim shadow over everything, it would have been a splendid time of both political and personal affirmation for Nellie. But casualties in Europe were mounting. The United States declared war, and with Jack already two years in the trenches, Nellie volunteered for the Red Cross. In its first year her branch made up $36,000 worth of care packages filled with bandages, underwear, toiletries, and chocolate to send to the front. But

Nellie still felt women weren't doing enough for the war effort.

⬡

There were only six women in the Edmonton branch of the Canadian Women's Press Club that morning. What used to be a delicious lunch with a variety of cakes and sandwiches was now reduced to brown bread with margarine and some strong tea, part of wartime austerity measures. Nellie sat among her peers, sipped her tea, and listened to the excited chatter around the table.

"The Women's Volunteer Reserve went up against seven returned soldiers in a target-shooting match and won handily," reported one woman.

"Vacant lots in the city are now being cleared and hoed. We'll be planting potatoes all across Edmonton for the effort," another claimed.

"Women are moving into all the vacant jobs and you'll never guess what they're wearing," another woman piped up. "Overalls! Not only must we do the work of men, it seems some women want to look like them, too."

Nellie held her silence. This war was taking such a toll. Women's natural instinct to nurture others was being lost to shooting weapons and carrying arms. Now women seemed to want to take over not only the roles but the appearance of their men, and there was something decidedly wrongheaded about that. Within herself, Nellie felt the underlying cause of the war was spiritual: humans seeking material gain, forgetting their responsibility to their neighbours and sinking deeper and deeper into sin. A change of heart, a change of attitude, the transforming power of a spiritual force was the only way the war would end.

Nellie bowed her head while the women talked around her. She saw polarity – two opposite extremes. While some women were bearing arms, wearing pants and training in reserve, a larger number were doing nothing but knitting scarves, a time-consuming task better suited to machines. Meanwhile, hundreds of rural schools were having to shut their doors for lack of teachers. Labour was short everywhere across the Prairies. Women could plow and harvest as well as men, women could teach, women could serve on the homefront. Knitting scarves wasn't the answer, but neither was taking on the posturing of men.

"We need real, full-sized women's jobs," Nellie responded to her assembled friends. "I think it's time Prime Minister Borden mobilized the women of the West. He may need a nudge or two, but we can't carry on as we are. It's time for action, ladies."

∞

She drafted and sent a letter to Prime Minister Borden, and within days of receiving it he invited Nellie and Judge Emily Murphy to be Alberta delegates at the Women's War Conference in Ottawa. There were a number of issues on the table the Albertans felt strongly about. They wanted all Canadian grain to be milled before being sent overseas to ensure it wasn't distilled into alcohol. They called for free technical training for women to allow them a larger role in the Canadian economy. They placed equal pay for equal work front and centre on the agenda, along with a minimum wage for working women. They also lobbied for a permanent group of female advisors to instruct government. And, for the most part, the federal government listened to the delegates and responded favourably.

"This is the first time the federal cabinet has ever sought the consultation of women," said Nellie to a fellow Western delegate. She stretched her feet out in front of her and watched the patchwork fields of early spring roll past the window of the train. "We have come a long way," she sighed, "and yet so much remains the same." Nellie closed her eyes, knowing full well that what was gained could just as easily be taken away.

∞

The war ended on November 11, 1918. Suddenly, women in factories, offices, and munitions plants were asked to step aside to make way for returning soldiers. This was like going back to washing clothes on two stones in a river after using an electric washer, Nellie said, and balked. She understood most women would gladly return to the safety of hearth and home, but she couldn't understand the almost total withdrawal of women from public affairs. "The independence of women is their greatest asset," she wrote in one of her speeches. "We are free to view the issues from a fresh, humanitarian point of view. Unlike men, we are not fretted by allegiance to either political party. If women merely lined up with the Liberals or the Conservatives, the only effect of our enfranchisement would be to double the voters list."

Instead, Nellie envisioned women voting on issues as a block. Like many Western reformers, she believed the old partisan parties were corrupted by patronage. Women would form their own opinions, regardless of party lines, she assumed. Their collective voice would result from weighing matters carefully, gathering evidence, listening to all sides with patience, understanding, and charity. "Women," wrote Nellie, "who are slow to think evil, ready to accord to each man his measure of praise, and then, act fearlessly, courageously, without favour, would become a terror to evildoers and a praise to them that do well."

But many women jumped ship, fled from the public domain to go home and tend to their men, who were staggering back to Canada beleaguered, wounded, and depressed. Nellie's unique brand of Christian Liberalism and her vision of a great body of women swaying government would have to wait. Her dream was sidelined and ignored. Her one consolation was Jack's return in March 1919.

∽

"Take off Jack's hat, Mark. It's too big for you," cajoled Wes, beaming at his two sons reunited at last. Jack was twenty-two when he returned from Europe. Mark was eight and heavily in the throes of hero worship. If Wes's concern was for their youngest son, Nellie's was for their eldest. Jack had returned to Edmonton a changed man. The war had taken the joy out of him and had matured him beyond his years. Paul and Horace felt the change most strongly. Who was this person, once their brother, now a stranger who walked around the house with the weight of the world on his shoulders? Jack sneered at their boyish pranks. He was far beyond boyhood – four years on the European front had seen to that – but he hadn't the maturity to bridge two worlds and accept that, back home, things had stayed relatively the same.

Nellie saw this and later tried to articulate on paper the immense pain she saw in her eldest child. "I knew there was a wound in his heart – a sore place," she wrote. "That hurt look in his clear blue eyes tore at my heart strings and I did not know what to do. When a boy who has never had a gun in his hands, never desired anything but the good of his fellow men, is sent out to kill other boys like himself, even at the call of his country, something snaps in him, something which may not mend."

Nellie realized the extent of Jack's pain when she overheard him speaking to a stranger near the back lane of their home.

The man, a large jocular fellow, approached Jack and extended his hand. "Well, young fellow," he said, pumping Jack's arm madly. "How does it feel to win a war?"

Jack dropped both his hand and his glance. "I did not know that wars were ever won," he replied in a soft, bitter-edged voice, keeping his eyes on the side-walk. He lifted his gaze, narrowing his eyes at the avuncular passerby. "If they are, it is certainly not by the people who do the fighting." With that, Jack turned on his heels and walked away, leaving the stranger speechless, cast adrift amid the trash barrels and uneven fences. Again, Nellie kept her counsel. Jack's injuries went far beyond the sprained fingers and bloody noses of his youth. These were hurts Nellie could not heal.

∞

William Lyon McKenzie King was elected leader of the federal Liberal party in 1919. Nellie McClung now had a new idol. Like her, King was a reformer. He was deeply religious and embraced the same sentimental religious ideals Nellie clung to. "Love Humanity" was King's credo, and nothing struck Nellie as more simple, more beautiful and more appropriate in a postwar world. Compromise, good will, faith, and reconciliation were Nellie's catch phrases, and when these same words tumbled out of the mouth of the national Liberal leader, Nellie was immediately won over.

Nellie read King's book, *Industry and Humanity*, in the wake of the 1919 Winnipeg General Strike, and it deeply impressed her. A new world order would not come through labour unrest and revolution – that was simply a manifestation of greediness – but through a welfare state where neighbour would look out for neighbour, rich would care for poor, power and wealth would be evenly distributed, not on the Marxist principals, but because people had opened their hearts to the love at the core of Christianity.

Nellie believed something similar to what King had written. And Nellie, who had long espoused non-partisan politics, decided at the outset of the 1921 election to let her name stand for the Liberal nomination in Edmonton. A brand-new political arm of the United Farmers of Alberta was forming a party, and its members were known as strong prohibitionists. In fact, their platform was co-operative and reformist, supporting many things Nellie had fought for over the years, but her allegiance to King and her past association with the Norris-led Liberal government in Manitoba was a tie too strong to break.

☙

"Why not run in a federal election, Nellie? There's a real need for your voice nationally. You already have a national profile, and I know you'd welcome the opportunity to work with King."

Agnes Laut, long-time friend of Wes and Nellie, was seated at their dining room table when she broached this question everyone had thought, but no one had dared speak.

Wes and Nellie exchanged glances, and, Agnes couldn't help but notice, small barely there smiles.

"Have you met our youngest son, Agnes?"

"Why yes. Young Mark."

"You see, while I'm flattered by the possibility of federal politics there is something that precludes my even thinking of it. My first duty is to my home and my family. Mark still needs a mother's constant care and love. I can serve people in Alberta without having to

leave home. That would not be possible if I were in
Ottawa. Would you like a sweet? "

∞

The new government, elected July 18, 1921, brought
great changes to the Alberta legislature. The Liberals
were swept from office, the Conservatives nearly oblit-
erated, and the dark horse, a party of unknown quan-
tity, the United Farmers of Alberta (UFA), took an easy
majority in the House with their occupation of thirty-
eight seats. Nellie didn't lose, but her party certainly
did. She was one of fifteen Liberals to form the
Opposition, but personal political victory was tempered
by the voters' obvious anti-Liberal sentiment. "Too
many good men and women have gone down to defeat
today for me to be bubbling over with joy at this time,"
Nellie said at her victory speech. "Perhaps the public
has a short-lived memory for services rendered."

Nellie was not the only woman in the Alberta
House of Assembly. The Honourable Irene Parlby
was elected for the UFA and soon became a cabinet
minister in the new government. She was the first
woman to serve as a cabinet minister in Alberta. In a
position of greater power, Parlby was able to push legislation through, while Nellie wasn't. At last ideologi-
cal beliefs about nonpartisan politics and the united
voice of women working together were translated into
action.

∞

The speaker was stout and stocky, an Independent in the House. His voice was deep and filled with righteous conviction. "I would like to ask why women, with husbands earning perfectly good wages, should hold positions in the marketplace and live in comfortable or luxurious circumstances when there are fine married family men out of work in our fair province? Should this be allowed?"

Across the floor from Nellie, Irene Parlby rose to her feet, incensed. "Mr. Speaker, I'm sorry, but women are recognized equally with men in regard to the laws, and in a free country no man should be allowed to legislate in such a discriminatory way against women."

Nellie also rose in support of her colleague. "It is strange that in spite of the progress of the last few years the impression still exists among men that every woman should be a housekeeper. Let women follow the calling they desire. I venture to guess that ninety percent of women do want to be housekeepers. But if a woman likes to teach school in preference to housekeeping and her conditions permit, then by all means, let her teach school."

Nellie sat. Irene rose again. Their eyes met. The House would hear more on this issue, and it mattered not which political party spoke. Women were not about to be legislated back into the home.

☙

The biggest disappointment Nellie faced during her four-year tenure as an MLA was the repeal of Prohibition. The argument put forward by a group called the Moderation League suggested legalizing the sale of liquor would eliminate the illegal and clandestine bootlegging operations. Prohibition, the group argued, kept drinkers at home, where women and children were most hurt.

A 51,000-name petition, launched by Alberta's hotelmen, was brought before the House. Despite Nellie's passionate pleas for temperance and her reminder that a high-minded, moral majority had worked long and hard to have the law enacted, Prohibition was overthrown. The same law that banned the sale of alcohol, the Direct Legislation Act, was amended to reinstate the sale of beer in Alberta in the summer of 1923. Shortly after, the province voted for the return of all liquour sales under government control.

Nellie was crushed. "We have slipped – we have failed – we have gone back and no one who has made an intelligent study of the question, and can see the question without prejudice, can have any feeling but sorrow."

The government of the day certainly felt no sorrow. Collectively the UFA opted not only to legalize both liquor sales and advertising, but also to run the stores at a profit. Yet, the political sting Nellie felt so keenly in public life was a mere annoyance compared to the trauma in her private life. In May, Wes was transferred to Calgary. Once the family arrived and had purchased a house on 7th Street West, and Nellie and Wes had worked out the commuting schedule between the capital and the southern city, he fell critically ill and was forced to go to a Banff sanatorium for treatment.

Nellie knew what she must do. She did not hesitate for a moment but took a leave of absence to spend time with Wes. "It was a case where duties conflicted, and I chose the one which is nearest and highest," she wrote to a friend.

Wes did recover and Nellie continued in politics, but a brief hiatus in Victoria, a three-month holiday prescribed by Wes's physician, gave the couple a chance to reassess their relationship. It also gave them a new perspective on their collective and individual energies. The McClungs were no longer young. Wes's illness was a wake-up call, a frightening glimpse of how life would be without the vigour and health they had so taken for granted in youth.

∞

Nellie faced the electorate one final time in Calgary in 1926, shortly after her return from the coast. Her campaign centred around criticism of the UFA's toothless liquor act and, of course, the rights of women. Because of her new residency, she had to stand for nomination in Calgary, a city where she was not well known.

It was 6 a.m. when Nellie awoke to the sound of the milk horse's hooves on cobblestones. The night before came rushing back. The election results had not been in when she'd fallen asleep. One Liberal candidate was soundly defeated, one was elected. There were only two seats to be had and her name hung in the balance. Today, this very morning, she would know.

Slipping out of bed so as not to wake Wes, Nellie padded barefoot to the window. The sun was just coming up, and the grass outside looked dewy and brilliant green. The two large elms in their backyard cast weird, filigree shadows on the lawn, like lacy black medallions. Nellie was suddenly reminded of looking out the window of the St. James house, years ago, with her older sister Hannah. Her memory was of Winnipeg, before the Mooney family had completed their own Western trek, before they had established their homestead, before the world of equality and Prohibition and the lovely loneliness of motherhood had opened up to her.

Two birds called to each other. Nellie looked back to the rumpled bed where Wes stirred. The unfinished business could not be put off. She went to the telephone, dialed, and waited. The final count of ballots, completed mere minutes ago, declared her unsuccessful in her bid for a second term as a Member of Alberta's Legislative Assembly.

"Though I went about quite lightheartedly and gay, telling myself and others how fine it felt to be free, and of how glad I was that I could go back to my own work with a clear conscience, there must have been some root of bitterness in me," reminisced Nellie, in her memoir. "I was seized with a desire to cook and I wanted the kitchen all to myself."

What followed was a total debauch of cooking.

"Mom! Telephone!"

"Let it go, Mark. I've jelly setting in the fridge and pastry to roll out. We'll just let the world go on without us today, shall we? I've pitted some dates. You can give the cat the last of the cream in that jar, and when you come back I should have a bowl for you to lick."

The baking didn't stop the insistent telephone, but Nellie blithely ignored calls of support and condolence. When the last of her pies was cooling on the windowsill and the blue and white kitchen was filled with good smells, a sense of peace and rightness descended. Wes came into the kitchen and put his arms around his wife. "Cooking soothes the troubled soul, but I've also brought you a gift."

Nellie frowned, wiping her flour-covered hands on her apron. Wes slowly opened his right hand. There was a new typewriter ribbon. Nellie looked at her husband and then at the small spool held in his large callused hand. Wes was offering her an invitation to leave the political world behind and get lost in the world of words. Nellie's eyes glazed over with tears. Sweet Wes. He was always right. In slanting afternoon light, in the blue and white Calgary kitchen, they embraced again. Something had ended. Something else had begun.

# 10

## *Famous 5 Chart a New Course*

*"We've known we were 'persons' all along."*
*– NLM*

And so Nellie wrote. Between 1923 and 1926 she published a novella and a novel and by 1931 had collected enough material to produce three more volumes of stories. Her characters sprang from the people around her, and in some ways were stock and stereotypical heroes and heroines. Elements of feminism and temperance almost inevitably surfaced in her fiction: frontier nurse confronts nasty bootlegger, shows him the evils of alcohol, reforms his ways, and, in typical happily-ever-after style, they wed, to begin a new life of service together.

A moment of personal triumph for Alberta's Famous 5 and a victory for women around the globe. Lord Chancellor Sankey delivers the Women are Persons Judgment in London, England, October 18, 1929.

An active member of the Canadian Authors Association, Nellie quickly established a Calgary branch and attended national and local conventions. Rubbing shoulders with authors like Sinclair Ross and Frederick Philip Grove, who both leaned towards true realism, Nellie was quick to defend her lighthearted style and the inevitable uplifting endings of her novels and stories.

" I think a writer should, above all things, faithfully portray life, and because there are more decent people than the other kind, it is keeping nearer to the truth to write of those who go right rather than those who go wrong. It is taking a mean advantage of the inoffensive reader to spring on him a story which depresses him or saddens him without purpose, weakening his faith in his fellow man," she wrote in her memoir. "The reader can get enough of that in life, he does not need to buy a book to get it." Nellie's unabashedly optimistic nature led her to emphasize a human being's ability to change for the better. "It is a serious thing to put pen to paper," she mused. "To have grace with the words carries responsibility."

While writing fiction kept her busy, Nellie admitted privately she was disillusioned with women's failure to live up to their enfranchisement. She saw women moving away from church duties, having smaller, often single-child families, and becoming occupied with idle pursuits such as bridge, tennis, and golf. "What Have We Gained In Sixty Years?", a 1927 essay for the *Canadian Home Journal*, expresses some of Nellie's regrets.

"A great many women are wandering in a maze of discontent and disillusionment," she wrote. "Idle hands and empty minds make an explosive mixture. Having little to do, they do nothing; and doing nothing, they miss that sense of work well done which sustained their grandmothers."

Without realizing it, Nellie herself was missing the dynamic energy of a good political battle. It wasn't long, however, before she received the call to take up the struggle once again.

∽

Nellie's opportunity to get back into the political fray arrived in the form of a letter from her old friend Emily Murphy. Murphy was eyeing admission to the Canadian Senate, the first time a woman dared dream herself into the judicious and patriarchal Upper House. She had asked that Nellie take up her cause in a letter-writing campaign. But like Murphy's attempts to request the appointment of a woman senator, Nellie's letters, first to Prime Minister Borden and later to Mackenzie King, were ignored. Further action was required, and Emily Murphy had a plan.

Section 24 of the British North America Act, 1867 (BNA Act) stated only "qualified persons" might be called to the Senate. In 1876, a British Court had decreed women "persons in matters of pain and penalties, but not persons in matters of rights and privileges." This flew in the face of everything Nellie and all suffragists had worked towards. The BNA Act had to be amended.

"They say time and careful thought are needed to amend the great foundations of our liberties," Murphy wrote to Nellie, "and while I agree constitutional change takes time, I believe I have found a more direct means of assault that will hasten the process of equality in the Chamber."

The letter went on to explain a loophole Murphy felt would hasten the feminist cause. Under section 60 of the Supreme Court Act, a clause stated any five interested citizens could band together and ask gov- ment for an interpretation of constitutional law. Murphy had the support of three other women. Would Nellie be interested in joining Henrietta Muir Edwards, expert on the legal status of Canadian women; Louise McKinney, WCTU leader; and her old parliamentary rival Irene Parlby to sign a petition? And if so, could she attend a planning session at Murphy's house on August 27, 1927, to prepare a petition?

Nellie leapt at the chance, and on the appointed day, after much haggling about wording, Nellie McClung added her signature to the document along-side the four others. In that final pen stroke, the group eventually known as Alberta's "Famous 5" was formed.

∽

Nellie spoke first. "The only real question is the meaning of the word 'persons.' Anything else simply confuses the issue." Three of the four petitioners agreed. Emily Murphy's three-question petition with its request for an interpretation of the BNA Act had been returned. Although the petition was accepted in principal, the wording of her question – "Is power vested in the Governor General of Canada, or the Parliament of Canada or either of them to appoint a female to the Senate of Canada?" – was not. Because the Canadian Parliament had no part in Senate appointments the petition would have to be rewritten.

Nellie knew that Emily didn't want to simplify the petition, but the wording of all three questions had been deemed either irrelevant or confusing by the government. "We should make it as plain and simple as possible," she mused. "The question we want addressed is this: Does the word 'persons' in section 24 of the British North American Act, 1867, include female persons? That's what we want to know. It couldn't be clearer."

Emily Murphy could do nothing but concede. The petition that would amend the BNA Act and make way for a female senator was close. Nellie, with advice from the Department of Justice, had named the defining issue. Plain talk, McClung style, eventually won Murphy over, and the reworded document with its five signatures was again sent to Ottawa.

The petition was heard by the Supreme Court of Canada in early March 1928. Longtime Ontario Liberal lawyer and suffrage supporter Newton Wesley Rowell argued on behalf of the five Alberta women against Solicitor General Lucien Caron and Quebec provincial representative Charles Lanctot. Six weeks later the verdict came down: Since at the time the BNA Act was signed no women held public office, the

Supreme Court concluded the Fathers of Confederation would not have intended women to be summoned to the Senate. In short, women could not be considered persons under the BNA Act.

Nellie and her cohorts were deeply disappointed but not totally surprised. Undaunted, they decided to go to the source. Murphy asked Rowell to appeal the Supreme Court decision to the Judicial Committee of the Privy Council in England. On July 22, 1929, Newton Rowell argued the "Persons" Case against Eugene Lafleur in London.

Three months later, to the joy of the five Albertans deemed "coal heavers and plough pushers" by their Eastern peers, quite a different decision was reached. On October 18, Lord Chancellor Sankey read his judgment: The BNA Act was planted in Canada as a living tree capable of growth and expansion within its natural limits. After much deliberation and review of various sections, the Privy Council was in favour of a liberal interpretation. The word "persons," therefore, is ambiguous and may refer to members of either sex, he concluded.

The five petitioners were exuberant at this victory, for they realized the implications of the decision furthered the public position of women throughout the British Empire. "We've known we were persons all along," quipped Nellie, speaking to the Women's Canadian Club of Calgary on January 22, 1930 at a celebration in honour of the five petitioners, "but it's now official. The findings of the Privy Council that we are 'persons,' once and for all, will do so much to merge us into the human family. I want to be a peaceful, happy, normal human being, pursuing my unimpeded way through life, never having to stop, to explain, defend or apologize for my sex."

∞

Despite her tireless reforms, Emily Murphy, with her stalwart Conservative family roots, was not chosen to be a senator. Nor was Nellie, despite strong Liberal leanings. The first Senate opening after the October 18, 1929 victory was in Ottawa, and the appointment was made on a geographic basis.

It is also possible Prime Minister King assumed the petitioners would be looking to shake up the placid Senate, and if so, he was likely right.

Cairine Wilson became the first woman appointed to the Canadian Senate. She was described by the press as "a lady of retiring disposition, of refinement and culture." Still, Nellie rejoiced. She knew Wilson as a human rights activist advocating Canada accept Jews fleeing Europe. It wasn't a popular stance but it was a stance Nellie agreed with. Reforms may not be happening as fast as she'd like, but gradually, one small victory at a time, the barriers were coming down. Women were taking their rightful place of power and opinion alongside their male counterparts.

# 11

## The Lantern Dims

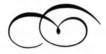

*"I want to write a book, in which many peo-
ple will find their own experiences, and I can
see that I am doing it." – NLM*

"Y ou can't go on like this. Your blood pressure is
high, indicating more strain on your heart, and
you can't tell me, in God's truth, these hands aren't
aching with arthritis."

Doctor's words. Doctor's orders. Nellie could do
nothing but listen. The time had come. She needed to
slow down. The year was 1932. Nellie was fifty-nine
years old, still in Calgary, still speaking, advocating,
challenging, and writing.

In 1936 Prime Minister McKenzie King appoints Nellie McClung
to the first Board of Broadcast Governors of the Canadian
Broadcasting Corporation (CBC). As the sole female voice
on the board, she advocates hiring women broadcasters and
keeping alcohol advertising off the airwaves, among other things.

Nellie and Wes (seated) surrounded by family and friends
on their golden wedding anniversary, August 25, 1946
at Lantern Lane, Gordon Head, B.C.

The ordination of women was her new battle-ground, and the Christian Church, "departed in some places from Christ's teachings, most noticeable in its treatment of women," her hidebound opponent.

But, like an answered prayer, Wes was offered a transfer to Victoria at the same time Nellie realized her energies were finite. The McClungs moved to Victoria without their children. Jack had finished his graduate studies at Oxford. Florence and her husband Hugh Atkinson were living in Regina. Paul had long been in Texas, where his fortunes had turned when he fell in love and married a young American girl, who produced the first of many McClung grandchildren. Horace, who was courting Calgary beauty Margaret Grace McNamara, decided to remain in the city, and young Mark, following in his eldest brother's scholastic foot-steps, was seeking university entrance. Like all their other community leave-takings, the farewell to Calgary left Nellie and Wes with a sense of sadness.

Change was invigorating, however, and the island city of Victoria presented a new landscape. The West Coast, with it's towering mountains, fog, and tangy sea air, offered Prairie people a new perspective. And, as Nellie quickly found out, people everywhere were drawn to her energy.

Despite her vow to give up public speaking, it was mere weeks before the invitations started to arrive at the McClungs' rented Victoria house. In a letter to a Calgary friend, Nellie admitted the pace hadn't neces-sarily slowed down, it had simply changed: "I spoke at two guest teas this week and will speak at one tomor-row. And I have two lectures to give. I think it is seven times I have addressed meetings, but I feel real well and am glad to be able to help a little."

Because Wes was to retire in 1933, the McClungs put down only temporary roots in Victoria. They were searching for their retirement home, and just as 1934 gave way to 1935 and hope was dimming, they finally found exactly what they were looking for.

∞

The morning dawned grey; a rough-wool-blanket day, stiffened by razor-blade winds.

"It's a difficult day to be enthusiastic about anything, isn't it my love?" asked Nellie, wrapping herself in her yellow rain slicker and preparing to leave the house. "I'm not feeling a lot of hope."

"It won't hurt to look," responded Wes. "The house is only six miles out of town at Gordon Head, and we will have a jaunt in the country if nothing else."

"How long has it been empty?"

"Some time now, so don't expect too much."

Bouncing along in the car, Nellie suddenly felt quite cheerful. "It is good to get out," she agreed, looking out the passenger window and admiring the way the land sloped to the southeast. Soon, a little lane appeared, and Wes steered between two rows of cherry trees. At the end of the lane they stopped and got out. The sea was close, the rank smell of seaweed and salt all around them. The outline of a dark green, shingled semi-bungalow lured them farther from the car, and as they walked towards the house, the clouds shifted and the sun peeked out.

"Wonderful," cried Nellie clasping her hands together. A single flood of light illuminated the little house and the land around it in a flash. It caught the bright red roof of a neighbouring house, briefly touched the wings of a windmill on a water tower below, and lit up the trees. That fleeting flood of light stole Nellie's heart and sold the grey green house. As the wooliness of the day rolled back over the couple, Nellie refused to see the bungalow as it was. The rain-soaked plaster and water pooling on the floor beneath a broken window were nothing compared to the light-filled landscape she had momentarily glimpsed.

"It's perfect," she cried, marking the straight floors, the pullied windows, and the three fireplaces to keep them warm. "It's just what we need." Once she had seen the house as it could be, in the light, Nellie was determined to have it.

"The sun porch will make an ideal study. I'll put bright draw curtains on that window and when I look up from my work, Wes, I shall see the ocean. What do you think, Wes? Shall we have it?"

With his wife as excited as a child, Wes could not bear to point out the bungalow's imperfections. Nor did he want to. The land around the house intrigued him. It was about ten hectares. He could have a market garden here. He could muck about outdoors in the garden for the rest of his life. "Yes, Nellie," said Wes. "Let's have it."

He put his arm around his wife's waist, and the two walked around the house, peering in each window and deep into the overgrown garden. Three weeks later, they moved in. Because no streetlights existed on the laneway, Wes hung a ship's lantern above the garage.

"To welcome our visitors," he said, admiring the way the soft glow penetrated the darkness and illuminated the narrow road.

"Lantern Lane," said Nellie. "We've come home."

∞

The move was a good one for both McClungs. Wes puttered in the garden, Nellie wrote; Nellie puttered in the garden, Wes mended things around the property. Contentment reigned. Shortly after their move Nellie recorded these words: "But to return to my onions. There they lie, the seeds I mean, under an inch of soil in rows fourteen inches apart, according to directions on the envelope, and when the rain falls now it will have a new meaning for me, for it will start the little hard seeds to geminate. And soon the little green threads will pierce the sod, and then no longer on government papers, or other place, will I need to give my occupation as *housewife*, that pallid name which no woman likes to own. I will boldly inscribe in that column this good strong word, *Onion-Grower!*"

∞

The same way she could not escape speaking at missionary teas in Victoria, Nellie could not escape political life. Through the thirties, she continued to lobby the newly formed United Church for the ordination of women. That her own church, the Methodist communion, lagged sadly behind in feminist reformed thinking galled Nellie. As early as 1921, when asked to be the sole female delegate to the Fifth Ecumenical Methodist Conference in England, she'd called for women's right to the pulpit. The issue quieted while unity was forged among the Methodist, Congregationalists, and Presbyterians in 1925, but three years later the United Church General Council quashed the ordination of it's first female candidate, Lydia Gruchy.

Nellie never let the Church forget. In an article published in *The Country Guide*, shortly after the Senate victory of the Famous 5, Nellie wrote: "Now with the Senate doors open there are only the two great institutions that will not accept women on equal terms, the church and the beer parlours."

The move to Lantern Lane didn't mean Nellie rested on her laurels, ignoring issues she believed in. From her study overlooking the sea she continued her fight for ordination of women, mostly through writing, and when at last it was obtained, and Lydia Gruchy brought into full fellowship with the United Church of Canada, Nellie used her wit and words to endorse the decision. In a widely published 1936 article, entitled "The Long Road to Freedom," Nellie wrote:

> The United Church of Canada took ten years to make up its mind whether or not it could allow a women to be ordained in its ministry. Only one application for ordination had been before the Council all these ten years. Miss Lydia Gruchy has a perfect record of eleven years in country service. Now she is to be ordained. So the United Church has at last

endorsed what Saint Paul said more than eighteen hundred years ago, that there is no male or female, bond or free, but all are one in the service of God.

∞

Nellie's love of God expressed itself in service to others. Her opinions, well thought-out and well written, were vented in a weekly column syndicated to newspapers across Canada. In this column Nellie deconstructed the cause of the Great Depression and admonished the Christian Church to do more for the masses of suffering unemployed. She dispensed wisdom and advice on many topics, from the psychological empowerment of social welfare programs, to a practical method of growing and distributing root vegetables to the less fortunate.

As the Second World War reared its ugly head and the Japanese dropped their bombs on Pearl Harbor, Nellie fought for the rights of interned Japanese Canadians. Her writing did not always make her popular, but as she confided to Wes, "I write what needs to be said."

∞

"Wes?"

"Yes, m'love?"

"King has asked me to sit on the board of governors for the Canadian Broadcasting Corporation."

"King?"

"Yes, Mackenzie King."

"That's an honour, Nell."

They were sitting by the fire in the front room, Nellie curled up with a book, Wes patiently feeding twigs into the crackling flames. He seemed to digest her news, and after a pause, he spoke again.

"Broadcasting?" He half turned on his stool and looked across the room at his wife, lovely in the half-light of the dim cottage. "Funny," he said, still warmed and amazed by Nellie's proud and gentle countenance, "I've always thought of you as a writer."

The Canadian Broadcasting Corporation (CBC) was a fledgling organization in 1936, but as one of its Board of Broadcast Governors, Nellie wanted to see national public radio fulfil two great mandates: namely, to weave together Canada's diverse population and use its people and their voice as interpreters in world relations and, quite simply, to educate. "Radio," she wrote in an article entitled 'The Voice of Canada', "is the greatest university in the world, with the lowest fees, the largest student body and the easiest manner of entrance."

Regionalism played its own role. Nellie wanted to make sure the West was heard. Her own people, adopted, fictionalized, or ancestral, needed their voice, and Nellie McClung lobbied hard to make sure they got it.

Despite deteriorating health, Nellie didn't immediately curtail her travelling. She used Lantern Lane as a retreat, a restful, calm oasis following many trips. In 1938, she was invited by the Women's Institute of Nova Scotia to speak at their Silver Jubilee celebration, followed by a speaking tour of the province. Nellie loved the people of the Maritimes and was particularly impressed by the co-operative housing movement that was sweeping the region. "It's Christianity's answer to communism," she told one woman from Reserve Mines, near Antigonish, who confessed ownership of a co-op house meant she would have not only her own vegetables and flowers but "a decent place to live, as well."

In principal, Nellie supported many political movements and she continued to endorse ideas outside party lines. She was excited by the platform of the Co-operative Commonwealth Federation (CCF), which had made its first appearance in federal politics three years earlier in 1935. She could not, however, divorce herself from the Liberals. "It would be far better for everyone if the Socialists had thrown their weight in with an already existing party of progressive-minded people," she wrote. "They seem to think that anyone who remains in either of the old parties [Liberals or Conservatives] is in the pay and service of the Big Interests."

Nellie was still somewhat naive. While on her Maritime tour she received another call from King. Would she be a member of the Canadian delegation to the League of Nations? Nellie was flattered. The girl who loved the limelight still existed within the wiser woman, and Nellie accepted the position despite a dire warning from friend and ex-delegate, Charlotte Whitton, who claimed Nellie should prepare to be "sickeningly disillusioned" by the international body.

The seas were finally calm. Nellie stretched out on a deck chair and wrapped the wool blanket firmly around her legs. Autumn was near and the sun weak, but she felt it full on her face and closed her eyes to its warmth. Her second Atlantic crossing had begun four days ago when the *Empress of Britain* sailed out of Quebec City. Soon they would land in Cherbourg, France and then the frantic schedule would start again. But now, in this lull between shores, on the great rolling expanse of the grey Atlantic, Nellie indulged in solitary thought.

Her mind drifted like the gulls that followed the ship, lighted on Lantern Lane, where Wes was harvesting and probably stewing over his carrot crop, then flew back to the CBC board. She was making such little headway in her campaign to hire female broadcasters. And the Maritimes! Such beautiful country, such warm people, such dire poverty. Nellie's brow furrowed.

Two major tasks lay ahead. She was to join the controversial Oxford Group at Interlaken for ten days of talks. Two thousand representatives from forty-five countries were gathering. Good people, in Nellie's mind, this group whose desire was to help and quicken all religious thought. They still believed the world could yet be changed and improved by the practice of God's will.

Perhaps the Oxford Group would bring God's control to a troubled world. Europe was in turmoil. Germany was governed by a powerful and aggressive man, Adolph Hitler, and as neighbouring countries crumbled under his power, he was taking them under his autocratic rule.

Opening her eyes and watching the horizon gently pitch, Nellie turned her thoughts to gentler matters. In Europe she would meet Mark, her baby boy, child of her middle years. He would come down from Oxford to spend time with her. Like his brother Jack, Mark was clever – a Rhodes Scholar. What a blessing. What a joy.

As the League of Nations was meeting in Geneva, she and Mark would travel together to Switzerland to see the Alps and bathe in the lakes. And at the League, Nellie imagined she and her colleagues would hammer out a plan for international peace. She smiled. The sun was warm, the way was bright, and despite her aching joints and the age that had stealthily crept up on her, she could still be useful.

The lulling motion of the ship through the water had its desired affect. On August 26, 1938, while the world stood at the threshold of a second great war, Nellie Letitia McClung, full of hope and faith in the future, dozed on the deck of the *Empress of Britain* in the lingering late summer sun.

∞

"The movement is called Moral Re-Armament. It calls on each of us as individuals to spend quiet time listening for God's instruction."

Wes sighed. "You needn't convert me, Nellie."

Glancing at her husband of almost fifty years, Nellie wrinkled her nose. "I was so disappointed with the League of Nations! There was no commitment to peace. Just hollow and self-serving words. The League lacked power, Wesley. And I mean the compelling, constraining power which comes into men's hearts when they love their neighbours as themselves, and know what concerns one, concerns all!"

"And you found this with the Oxford Group, or, what are they now? The Moral Re-Armament Group?"

"Yes. The difference between Interlaken and the League of Nations is the difference between hope and fulfilment. At Interlaken I saw the Christian message in action. Rich and poor, bishops and communists, coal miners and university professors, all united in one purpose – to know the will of God and do it."

Wes, thoughtful, ever patient, paused before he spoke. " There is a war now, Nellie. The Moral Re-Armament movement has been associated with the Nazis. Perhaps it's not a good time to espouse their philosophies."

"The Golden Rule? The Grace of God? The Good Neighbour Policy? What do you mean, not a good time?"

And, as in days gone by, the McClungs engaged in a heated theological argument.

Her body, her mortal shell, was ultimately what slowed Nellie McClung. At the Board of Broadcast Governors' meeting in Ottawa on November 10, 1940, shortly after her impassioned plea to suspend advertising of liquor on public radio, Nellie suffered a near-fatal heart attack. The attack felled her body, grown stout with years, but not her indomitable optimism. "When my brain cleared I was left with a great longing to live," she wrote. "The age of plenty is here, if only the heart of man can be prepared, and he can be made to see that what hurts one nation, hurts all. What a time to be alive! So I lived!"

At sixty-seven, with her heart severely deteriorated, Nellie knew time was of the essence. She didn't have long and there was still so much left to do. She quit her post at CBC and resigned from her weekly column. Nellie now tackled the one manuscript that most needed to be finished, her autobiography. She'd started to write it in 1933 "before all the colours faded from the canvas of my life," but halted at the moment she and Wes were married.

*Clearing in the West* told the story of the young Nellie, the vibrant life of Prairie pioneers and the harsh landscape she and her family claimed as their own. It didn't touch on the evolution of political parties, the enfranchisement of women – the issues, real, absorbing, and vital, that mattered so much to the mature Nellie.

She set to the task immediately, recognizing the brevity of life. *The Stream Runs Fast*, part two of Nellie McClung's life, was published in 1945, but it was a changed and depleted Nellie who went to that celebratory autograph session. During the pleasant task of recording her life's work, Nellie suffered her worst and cruelest blow.

∞

Ashen-faced, shaking, with the clay of the earth still on his large hands, Wes came to her on February 17, 1944.

"Nellie."

She looked up from her work and knew something terrible had happened.

"It's Jack."

Nellie half rose. "Jack?"

"There's been a call. He's dead, Nell. Our boy is dead." The stiff-upper-lip training of his youth could not keep the tremor from John Wesley McClung's voice. Heart shattered, he went to his wife, knelt, and sobbed into her lap.

"What do you mean, Wes? Jack? Dead? No... no... that's impossible. Jack is in Edmonton. What are you telling me?"

And in the quiet of a dim February evening, with the fog heavy on the land and the horns of Gordon Head howling their mournful warning, Nellie learned her firstborn boy had probably died by his own hand.

The details of Jack McClung's death are sketchy. He was a successful prosecuting attorney for the Alberta department of justice when his name became attached to a scandal. Funds had been mishandled. Jack McClung may have felt responsible. He signed over his pension to the government to make restitution for the misappropriated funds, but it is likely remorse and shame – Nellie McClung's son, associated with corruption – that played a role in his tragic and untimely death. In part, Nellie blamed herself.

"Was I too hard on him? Did I expect too much?" she lamented in the dark days that followed, as the family gathered and wept together. Horace's wife Margaret, who was assisting with the writing of the autobiography, knew how deeply Nellie was pierced. "I'm afraid for your mother, Horace," she confided to her husband. "She is very silent."

Nellie was silent, but as a writer she worked out some of her pain on the blank pages of her manuscript and, more personally, in her private journal. In *The Stream Runs Fast* she wrote, "I knew there was a wound in his heart, a sore place... like a wound in a young tree. It does not grow out. It grows in." Jack's war experience – the horrors of what he saw as a young man – put that wound there, according to Nellie. He'd tried to obliterate that vision but it had contributed to his death. Despite a lifetime of trying, Nellie had been unable to save her firstborn.

∞

"The disciples on the road to Emmaus were blind to their Lord when he returned."

"Yes, Nellie"

"They were blind to His resurrection and eternal life until they recognized Him in His action of blessing and breaking the bread."

"Yes."

"We must hold on to that Wes. *They knew him in the breaking of bread.*"

"Ahhh..."

Nellie studied her husband's face. The thinning red hair, the once bright blue eyes, now so filled with sorrow. In her raw pain, Nellie clung to her faith and she wanted to comfort: "Death is not the end. It is but the portal to a brighter, fairer world."

Wes nodded, but Nellie continued: "The part we see with our mortal eye does not make sense; it is like the fragment of a story you read in a torn magazine, you know there must be more of it."

Recalling her childhood, Nellie resolved to overcome her sorrow by continuing with the work at hand. In 1945, she published *The Stream Runs Fast* and began to formulate plans for a new novel.

∞

Sunday, August 25, 1946, dawned clear and bright. Nellie and Wes were celebrating their golden wedding anniversary, fifty years of marriage. Both somewhat frail, the couple happily welcomed four of their five grandchildren, three of their remaining four children, and various spouses and family friends to their home on Lantern Lane. Horace, like all the McClung children, had the gift of doggerel verse. He opened the celebration in the garden with: "Fifty years ago this day/ Mama wouldn't say obey…"

Laughter rang though the trees and across the expanse of lawn. Nellie and Wes kissed each other. "I still consider the day I cut him out of the herd the best day of my life," she later wrote to one of Wes's colleagues.

∞

Nellie lived six more years, but her pain increased and her energy decreased. Although required to rest for longer and longer periods, she lost none of her wit or spirit. A few years before her death, a member of the Canadian Authors Association interviewed Nellie McClung at Lantern Lane. Nellie was sitting in a sunny corner of the yard, sheltered by a hedge. A book lay open on her lap. Wes's flowers were at their height, and birds whistled and sang from a nearby orchard.

"You look so well, Mrs. McClung," said the young researcher. "It's lovely here, isn't it?" He sighed and sat, drawing up a chair beside Nellie.

"If I were only a few years younger, I'd move tomorrow to Winnipeg with its blizzards," Nellie replied, deadpan.

∞

Nellie Letitia McClung died on September 1, 1951, just before her seventy-eighth birthday. Two days earlier, as she lay still on her bed, Wes had leaned over, unsure if he'd feel her faint breath on his cheeks. With a little twitch, Nellie opened her eyes. "Oh, I'm still here! I'll never believe I'm dead till I see it in the papers." Wes smiled through his tears. His wonderful Nell.

Nellie's death, when it came, was gentle. Her funeral, four days later, was simple. Her own pastor spoke a graveside eulogy, and while reminding the McClung family and friends of the promises of Christ, he was overcome with emotion.

As the word of her death spread across Canada, Nellie was well remembered in the press. An editor of the *Family Herald and Star Weekly* wrote: "Nellie McClung developed into, and remained, a person who attracted love from all who knew her and yet inspired them with respect for her vigorous strength of character... it was the four old-fashioned virtues of simplicity, sincerity, courage, and intelligence which combined to make Nellie McClung respected and feared as a fighter for the causes of temperance and women's rights... a sort of unofficial 'No. 1 Woman of Canada.'"

Mark, who at his mother's insistence did not attend her funeral, found a more personal comfort reading one of Nellie's books. In *The Next of Kin*, Nellie wrote her own version of death: "We know there is a future state, there is a land where the complication of this present world will be squared away. Some call it a day of judgement; I like best to think of it as a day of explanations... Also I know we shall not have to lie weary centuries waiting for it. When the black curtain of death falls on life's troubled scenes, there will appear on it these words in letters of gold, *End of Part I. Part II will follow immediately*."

With those words, the sassy actor and writer, the passionate activist, the social reformer – the woman who was a friend to all and who changed the lives of many – took her final bow.

The Calgary Monument of the Famous 5 in Olympic Plaza was unveiled on October 18, 1999 – the seventieth anniversary of the "Persons" Case. Nellie McClung holds the newspaper proclaiming *Women are Persons!* Sculptor: Barbara Paterson. Monument donors: Ann McCaig and daughters Roxanne & Jane; Dr. Maria Eriksen & Ayala Manolson; Kiki Delaney; Senator Vivienne Poy; Heather Reisman.

# Chronology of Nellie McClung (1873-1951)

*Compiled by Lynne Bowen*

| McClung and Her Times | Canada and the World |
|---|---|
| **1812**<br>John Mooney (father) is born in Ireland. | |
| | **1816**<br>In British North America, rivalry between the Hudson's Bay Company (HBC) and the North West Company and disputes over pemmican and the Métis culminate in the Seven Oaks incident; after the two companies merge in 1821, the Métis become a permanent element in the Red River Settlement. |
| **1830**<br>John Mooney arrives in Canada. | |

| McClung and Her Times | Canada and the World |
|---|---|
| **1832**<br>Letitia McCurdy (mother) is born in Dundee, Scotland. | |
| **1841**<br>John Mooney moves to Grey County, Ontario. | **1841**<br>Upper and Lower Canada unite to form the Province of Canada and become Canada West and Canada East respectively. |
| | **1849**<br>Henrietta Edwards née Muir (future member of the Famous 5) is born in Montreal. |
| | **1853**<br>Rodmond Palen Roblin (future premier of Manitoba) is born in Sophiasburg, Canada West. |
| **1858**<br>Widower John Mooney meets Letitia McCurdy, an immigrant from Scotland, in Bytown (Ottawa); she becomes his second wife and moves into his farmhouse on Garafraxa Road, 1.5 kilometres south of Chatsworth, Grey County, Canada West. | |
| **1859**<br>William "Will" Mooney (brother) is born. | |
| **1861**<br>George Mooney (brother) is born. | **1861**<br>Tobias Crawford Norris (future premier of Manitoba) is born in Brampton, Canada West. |

| McClung and Her Times | Canada and the World |
|---|---|
| **1867**<br>Elizabeth "Lizzie" Mooney (sister) is born. | **1867**<br>Under the British North America (BNA) Act, Canadian Confederation unites Canada West (Ontario), Canada East (Quebec), Nova Scotia, and New Brunswick. |
| **1868**<br>Jack Mooney (brother) is born. | **1868**<br>In Rupert's Land, Louis Riel returns from working in the United States (U.S.) to live in the Red River Settlement.<br><br>Emily Murphy née Ferguson is born in Cookstown, Ontario; Louise McKinney née Crummy is born in Frankville, Ontario; Irene Parlby née Marryat is born in England; all three are future members of the Famous 5. |
| | **1870**<br>Louis Riel orders the execution of Thomas Scott; Ottawa sends soldiers on a "mission of peace"; Riel flees to the U.S.<br><br>The Manitoba Act creates Canada's fifth province; it recognizes French and English as official languages and allows funding of Protestant and Catholic schools by public taxation; quarter sections of land are opened for settlement. |
| **1871**<br>Hannah Mooney (sister) is born. | **1871**<br>Donald Smith becomes the chief commissioner of the HBC and Member of Parliament for Selkirk. |

*Nellie McClung*

| McClung and Her Times | Canada and the World |
|---|---|
| **1873** <br> Nellie Letitia Mooney is born on October 20th in Grey County, Ontario. | **1873** <br> American suffragist Susan B. Anthony is tried for attempting to vote; the judge refuses to allow her to testify, dismisses the jury, and finds her guilty. |
| | **1874** <br> The first Canadian branch of the Women's Christian Temperance Union (WCTU) is formed in Owen Sound, Ontario. |
| | **1876** <br> In Canada, Dr. Emily Stowe founds Canada's first suffrage group. <br><br> In Britain, a court interprets the BNA Act to say that women are "persons in matters of pain and penalties, but not persons in matters of rights and privileges." |
| **1879** <br> In May, Will Mooney and his friend Neil Macdonald go "out West" to find land for their families; they winter in the Souris Valley, where Will stakes a claim for his father, his brother George, and himself. | |
| **1880** <br> The Mooney family sells most of its belongings and travels via steamer from Owen Sound to Duluth and on to Manitoba where they rent a house in St. James near Winnipeg for the women while the men go to the homestead to build | **1880** <br> In the U.S., the federal government appoints Select Committees on Woman Suffrage in the House and Senate. |

## McCLUNG AND HER TIMES

a log house; in September the family moves into the new home southeast of the Brandon Hills.

### 1881
Lizzie Mooney is gravely ill; Methodist minister Reverend Thomas Hall arrives just in time with medicine to save her life.

### 1882
The Mooney family builds a new house; a schoolhouse is built two miles away at Northfield; the neighbours give the family a chicken shower after a weasel kills twenty-six of their hens.

### 1883
When Nellie tells a lie about her dog, Nap, she learns a lesson that she will always remember; Nellie and Hannah start school in Northfield.

### 1884
Jack and Letitia criticize Nellie for being forward when she pours tea for some men at the Black Creek stopping house where the family has stopped en route to Brandon.

### 1885
Nellie and Hannah prepare a written report on Riel and the Métis in the Northwest Rebellion for a school project; Nellie learns of Riel's hanging by reading the Brandon and Montreal newspapers.

## CANADA AND THE WORLD

### 1881
In the past five years, 40,000 immigrants, mainly of British stock from Ontario, have settled in Manitoba; the province's borders are extended.

### 1882
In Canada, the thirty-eight-year-old *Globe* newspaper adds a women's section to its pages; the Canadian Pacific Railway (CPR) reaches Brandon, Manitoba.

### 1884
In Canada, Louis Riel moves to Batoche in the Saskatchewan Valley to help the Métis obtain their legal rights.

### 1885
In Canada, the Northwest Rebellion breaks out when Riel's men clash with the North West Mounted Police at Duck Lake in the District of Saskatchewan; the newly built CPR transports soldiers to the Prairies; Riel is

## McClung and Her Times

## Canada and the World

arrested and charged with treason; he is tried, found guilty, and appeals his sentence; public pressure from Quebec delays the execution, but Riel is finally hanged on November 7th.

Elsewhere in Canada, Donald Smith drives the last spike of the CPR; the national WCTU is organized to campaign for Prohibition and to promote female suffrage, sex hygiene, and mothers' allowances.

### 1889

Nellie passes the entrance exams for Normal School with top marks; she moves to Winnipeg for the five-month course.

### 1889

In Canada, Emily Stowe becomes the first president of the Dominion Women's Enfranchisement Association.

### 1890

Nellie's term at Normal School ends in February; she goes home with her second-class teaching certificate.

Nellie leaves home in August by train and travels to the Hazel School near Manitou to take up her teaching position; she organizes a Christmas concert for the entire community and, the following day, raises the spirits of her fellow passengers in a blizzard-bound train.

### 1890

In Manitoba, the Liberal government passes the Manitoba Schools Act, which halts public funding to Roman Catholic schools.

### 1891

Nellie's Bible School teacher at the Manitou Methodist church is the minister's wife, Annie McClung; Annie introduces Nellie

### 1891

Sir John A. Macdonald, Canada's first prime minister, dies in Ottawa.

## McClung and Her Times

to the cause of suffrage and supports her in her fight against the evils of liquor.

### 1892
Nellie completes her term at Hazel School and moves into Manitou to teach there; she meets Annie's eldest son, Robert Wesley "Wes" McClung.

Nellie establishes a literary society, joins the WCTU, writes short fiction, and becomes friends with E. Cora Hind, a journalist with the *Winnipeg Free Press*.

### 1893
John Mooney dies in January.

In December, Nellie leaves Manitou and goes to Winnipeg to study for her first-class teaching certificate; she and her sister, Hannah, board together.

### 1894
Nellie completes her teaching certificate in August and accepts a school in Treherne, where the McClung family has just been transferred; she boards with the McClungs and writes often to Wes, who is managing two drugstores in Manitou.

### 1895
Because her mother needs her help during harvest, Nellie stays home to cook for the crew; she

## Canada and the World

### 1893
In Canada, Henrietta Edwards helps Lady Aberdeen, wife of the Governor General, found the National Council of Women.

### 1895
In Canada, Manitoba refuses to obey the court order to reopen Catholic schools.

| McCLUNG AND HER TIMES | CANADA AND THE WORLD |
|---|---|

worries about losing her dream of being a writer if she marries.

**1896**
Still living with her mother, Nellie begins to teach school at North-field School; Wes comes to meet her family.

**1896**
Liberal Wilfrid Laurier becomes Canada's first prime minister of French Canadian ancestry.

Nellie marries Wes McClung on August 25 and they set up their home in a flat over the Manitou drugstore.

**1897**
Nellie McClung gives birth to her first child, John Wesley (Jack) on June 16.

**1897**
In response to French opposition to the Manitoba Schools Act, the Manitoba Liberal government passes an amendment that provides for bilingual schools wherever ten or more students speak French or another non-English language.

In Ottawa, Henrietta Edwards helps Lady Aberdeen found the Victorian Order of Nurses.

**1898**
In Canada, temperance receives the largest number of votes in a national plebiscite, but Prime Minister Laurier says it is not a large enough majority to warrant passing a law prohibiting the sale of alcohol.

**1899**
Florence, Nellie McClung's only daughter, is born.

**1899**
The world's first Peace Conference is held in The Hague, in the Netherlands.

**McClung and Her Times**

**1900**
Temperance supporters, including Nellie McClung, boycott Premier Roblin's Prohibition plebiscite; in a campaign to persuade the people of Manitou to accept Prohibition, Nellie McClung and others take several petitions to cabinet but each one is dismissed as flawed.

**1901**
Nellie McClung gives birth to a son, Paul.

**Canada and the World**

During his brief term as Conservative premier of Manitoba, Hugh John MacDonald delights temperance advocates by bringing in the Liquor Act; the bill is not enforced.

**1900**
Businessman Rodmond Roblin becomes Conservative premier of Manitoba; a plebescite rejects Prohibition, and the Liquor Act is repealed, leaving individual municipalities to decide whether they want Prohibition.

Most women in Canada who own property are now allowed to vote in municipal elections.

In the U.S., the states of Wyoming, Utah, Colorado, and Idaho have given women full suffrage.

New Zealand is the first nation to grant women suffrage.

**1901**
Emily Murphy's book *The Impressions of Janey Canuck* is published.

**1903**
In Britain, Emmeline Pankhurst founds the National Women's Social and Political Union.

In Canada, Louise McKinney helps to organize the North-West Territories Branch of the WCTU.

# Nellie McClung

| McClung and Her Times | Canada and the World |
|---|---|
| | **1904**<br>James Shaver Woodsworth (future leader of the Co-operative Commonwealth Federation) works with immigrant slum dwellers in Winnipeg's All People's Mission and advocates the Social Gospel.<br><br>The Canadian Women's Press Club is founded. |
| **1906**<br>Horace, Nellie McClung's fourth child, is born. | **1906**<br>Finland gives women full suffrage. |
| **1907**<br>The audience at a WCTU convention receives Nellie McClung's first public speech with enthusiastic applause. | **1907**<br>American Harriet Stanton Blatch founds the Equality League of Self-Supporting Women, later called the Women's Political Union. |
| **1908**<br>Nellie McClung's *Sowing Seeds in Danny* is published and becomes a national bestseller. | **1908**<br>International Women's Day is celebrated for the first time.<br><br>Frank Buchman, disillusioned founder of a hospice for destitute young men in Philadelphia, goes to England and undergoes a religious experience which eventually leads to the formation of the Oxford Group. |
| **1909**<br>E. Cora Hind comes for an eight-day visit with Nellie McClung and comments on the many demands on Nellie's time and energy. | **1909**<br>The United Farmers of Alberta (UFA) is established in Edmonton to further rural economic, social, and political issues. |

## McClung and Her Times

## Canada and the World

J.S. Woodsworth's book *Strangers Within Our Gates*, which draws attention to the plight of immigrants in Canada, is published by the Methodist Church.

### 1910
Nellie's book *The Second Chance* is published.

### 1910
In Canada, the National Council of Women speaks out in favour of women's suffrage.

### 1911
Afflicted by what his wife calls "primitive Methodist conscience," Wes McClung finds business too stressful; he sells the drugstores, buys two farms with the proceeds, and rents them to tenants; in August the McClungs move to Winnipeg so Wes can sell life insurance; Nellie McClung has a writing room in their new house; she gives birth to another son, Mark, in October.

At a meeting of the Canadian Women's Press Club, Nellie McClung hears Mrs. Pankhurst, who is visiting from Britain, speak about the plight of the non-Anglo-Saxon female workers in Winnipeg.

### 1911
In Canada, Sir Wilfrid Laurier loses the federal election to Conservative Robert Borden; the main issue is free trade with the U.S.; in return for the support of Manitoba premier Rodmond Roblin, Borden extends the boundaries of Manitoba and recommends Roblin for a knighthood.

In the U.S., the National Association Opposed to Woman Suffrage is founded.

### 1912
Having tricked Premier Roblin into a visit to a factory where immigrant women work in appalling conditions, Nellie McClung and Mrs. Claude Nash report back to the Press Club.

### 1912
In the U.S., suffrage referendums are passed in Arizona, Kansas, and Oregon.

The *S.S. Titanic* sinks.

## McClung and Her Times

Nellie McClung and fourteen others establish the Women's Political Equality League in order to gether information on the status of women in Canada; women's rights and suffrage become Nellie McClung's new focus, but it is difficult to convince many in society, including many women.

Nellie's book *The Black Creek Stopping House* is published.

## Canada and the World

**1913**
British suffragettes demonstrate in London; Mrs. Pankhurst is jailed for inciting persons to place explosives.

Canadian Alice Jamieson is appointed judge of a juvenile court in Calgary and becomes the first woman appointed to any judiciary in the British Empire.

**1914**
The Political Equality League asks the Manitoba legislature for voting rights for women and is turned down; the League presents a mock parliament with Nellie McClung posing as Premier Roblin.

Despite media criticism regarding her "neglect" of her children, Nellie tours Manitoba campaigning for the Liberals, who have agreed to support giving women the vote and the right to run for elected office; the Liberals are defeated in the July election.

**1914**
Britain declares war on Germany; Canada is automatically at war; young men flock to join the armed forces.

In Canada, proponents of the Social Gospel advocate Prohibition, women's suffrage, civil service reform, and co-operatives.

## McClung and Her Times

The McClungs are vacationing when war is declared in Europe.

Seeing anew the effects of drunkenness, Nellie McClung and her political allies march on the legislature in October to demand temperance legislation; Roblin orders his Tories to leave the House.

### 1915
When her husband is offered a transfer by his employer, Nellie McClung turns her back on a possible cabinet post in a future Liberal government in Manitoba and agrees to move to Edmonton; she joins the Edmonton Equal Franchise League and allies herself with Emily Murphy and Alice Jamieson.

Nellie's book *In Times Like These* is published; she is keynote speaker at a temperance rally in British Columbia; on a speaking tour of Ontario her reputation is unjustly challenged in the press.

The temperance movement in Alberta forces a plebiscite; Nellie McClung marches with 1200 women down Edmonton's main street on the day before the July election; the majority vote for Prohibition.

Nellie McClung goes to Manitoba to campaign for the Liberals, who promise a women's suffrage bill; they win the election in August.

## Canada and the World

### 1915
T. C. Norris defeats Sir Rodmond Roblin in the Manitoba election.

In the Netherlands, the Women's International League for Peace and Freedom is founded in The Hague by women wishing to end war for all time.

In Denmark, women gain the right to vote.

# Nellie McClung

Eighteen-year-old Jack McClung enlists.

## 1916

Nellie McClung, Emily Murphy, and Alice Jamieson celebrate by buying new hats and having a photograph taken on the day Alberta women receive the vote and right to run for office.

Following enthusiastic reception of her speech to the National Women's Suffrage Association, Nellie McClung is invited on a six-week, forty-city tour of the U.S.; her daughter, Florence, accompanies her.

Although Nellie McClung does volunteer work for the Red Cross, she feels that women can do more to help the war effort by taking on proper jobs.

## 1916

In Canada, women receive the right to vote and run for provincial office in Manitoba on January 27, in Saskatchewan on March 14 and in Alberta on April 19; Manitoba passes the first mothers' allowance legislation in the country; the first female police magistrate in the British Empire, Emily Murphy, is appointed in Edmonton, and Alice Jamieson is appointed to a similar post in Calgary.

At the Battle of Vimy Ridge in April, Canadian soldiers fight as a unit for the first time and achieve victory where the British and French have failed.

Conscription divides Canadians along French/English lines and leads to the formation of the Union government, which offers the vote to the female relatives of soldiers.

In the U.S., Jeanette Rankin becomes the first woman to be elected to the House of Representatives.

## 1917

Nellie McClung's book *The Next of Kin* is published

## 1917

In Canada, Ontario women are given the vote in provincial elections; women in British Columbia receive the right to vote and run for provincial office; Louise

## MᶜCLUNG AND HER TIMES

## CANADA AND THE WORLD

McKinney is elected to the Alberta legislature; she is the first woman to be elected by both men and women in the British Empire. McKinney, Emily Murphy, and Henrietta Muir Edwards push for the passage of the Dower Act; in Ottawa, a national coalition government pledged to enact conscription and votes for women is formed.

The U.S. declares war on Germany and sends troops to Europe.

### 1918
In February, Prime Minister Borden invites Nellie McClung and Emily Murphy to represent Alberta at the Women's War Conference in Ottawa.

Nellie's book *Three Times and Out: A Canadian Boy's Experience in Germany* is published.

### 1919
Jack McClung returns from military service a world-weary man at the age of twenty-two.

Nellie McClung is deeply impressed with William Lyon Mackenzie King's book *Industry and Humanity*.

### 1918
The First World War ends on November 11; over eight million have died and twenty-one million have been wounded; a world-wide influenza epidemic begins that will kill almost twenty-two million people in two years.

In Canada, women over thirty get the vote; the federal government stops the manufacture and importation of alcohol into provinces where it is illegal.

### 1919
In Canada, women now can be candidates in federal elections; Ontario women receive the right to run for provincial office; when thirty thousand Winnipeg workers leave their jobs in a general strike, federal troops occupy the city and arrest several labour leaders; William Lyon Mackenzie King becomes leader of the federal

Liberal party; Quebec rejects Prohibition and attracts huge numbers of tourists as a result.

At the Paris Peace Conference, the Treaty of Versailles is signed and the League of Nations meets; among the delegates from Canada is Newton Rowell, a former Union government cabinet minister who is an advocate of conscription and a program of social insurance.

Lady Astor is the first woman elected to the British Parliament.

**1920**
Canada joins the League of Nations; British Columbia voters reject Prohibition.

In the U.S., women are finally given the vote; Prohibition is enacted.

**1921**
Nellie McClung's book *Purple Springs* is published.

The sole female delegate to the Fifth Ecumenical Methodist Conference in England, Nellie McClung calls for the ordination of women.

Although she agrees with much of the UFA platform, Nellie McClung runs for a seat in the Alberta legislature as a Liberal because of her ties to the Manitoba and federal Liberals; she becomes a member

**1921**
In Canada, the UFA wins the Alberta election; Irene Parlby (Alberta) and Mary Ellen Smith (British Columbia) become the first female cabinet ministers in the British Empire; Agnes Macphail becomes the first woman elected to the Canadian Parliament.

The Canadian Authors Association is founded in Montreal.

**McClung and Her Times**

of the Opposition when the UFA wins the election.

**1923**
The McClung family moves to Calgary, and shortly afterward Wes becomes sick and goes to a sanatorium in Banff; Nellie McClung takes a leave of absence from the legislature.

Nellie McClung's novella *When Christmas Crossed "The Peace"* is published.

**1925**
Nellie McClung's novel *Painted Fires* is published.

**1926**
Nellie McClung runs for a seat in the Alberta legislature in a Calgary riding, but loses the election.

**1927**
Nellie McClung's essay "What Have We Gained in Sixty Years?" is published in the *Canadian Home Journal*.

**Canada and the World**

**1923**
In Alberta, the Direct Legislation Act is amended to allow the sale of beer; in Manitoba the government takes over the sale and control of alcohol.

**1924**
Alberta and Saskatchewan vote for the return of the sale of all alcoholic beverages, under government control.

**1925**
In Canada, the United Church is formed from a union of the Methodist, Presbyterian, and Congregational churches; Frederick Philip Grove's book *Settlers of the Marsh* is published.

**1927**
Ontario and New Brunswick governments assume control of the sale of alcohol.

## MCCLUNG AND HER TIMES

## CANADA AND THE WORLD

Emily Murphy asks Nellie McClung to meet with her and Henrietta Edwards, Louise McKinney, and Irene Parlby to prepare a petition to the Supreme Court regarding the definition of "persons."

### 1928
In March, lawyer Newton Wesley Rowell on behalf of Nellie McClung and her four associates takes the first petition in the "Persons" case to the Supreme Court of Canada; the court says that the BNA Act does not consider women to be "persons."

### 1928
The United Church of Canada quashes the ordination of its first female candidate, Lydia Gruchy.

### 1929
Now known as Alberta's "Famous 5," Nellie McClung and her associates petition the Judicial Committee of the Privy Council (JCPC) in London, England in July; in October, the JCPC reverses the Supreme Court of Canada's 1928 decision in the "Persons" Case.

### 1929
With the collapse of the U.S. Stock Exchange on October 24, the ten-year-long Great Depression begins.

### 1930
Nellie McClung's book *All We Like Sheep* and her collection of sketches, stories, and poems *Be Good to Yourself* are published.

### 1930
The Nova Scotia government takes over the control and sale of alcohol.

Cairine Wilson is the first woman appointed to the Canadian Senate.

### 1931
Nellie McClung's collection of short fiction, *Flowers for the Living*, is published.

### 1931
The Women's International League for Peace and Freedom initiates a petition campaign for universal disarmament.

*Voice for the Voiceless*

## McCLUNG AND HER TIMES

**1932**
Although she is still active and is fighting for the ordination of women, Nellie McClung is not in good health; she and Wes move to Victoria, but she does not slow down.

**1933**
The McClungs begin to search for a house of their own after Wes retires.

**1935**
Nellie McClung's first autobiography, *Clearing in the West*, is published.

The McClungs finally find their retirement home in Gordon Head near Victoria; they name it "Lantern Lane."

**1936**
Nellie McClung is appointed to the Canadian Broadcasting Corporation's first Board of Broadcast Governors.

Nellie McClung's anthology of newspaper columns, *Leaves from Lantern Lane*, is published; her

## CANADA AND THE WORLD

**1933**
In Canada, Emily Murphy dies in Edmonton; the Co-operative Commonwealth Federation (CCF) is founded under the leadership of J.S. Woodsworth.

Prohibition is repealed in the U.S.

Nazi leader Adolf Hitler is appointed German Chancellor; Franklin Roosevelt is sworn in as President of the U.S.

**1936**
In Canada, Newton Rowell is appointed Chief Justice of Ontario; the United Church finally allows the ordination of Lydia Gruchy.

Mussolini and Hitler proclaim the Rome-Berlin Axis; King Edward VIII ascends the British throne,

## McClung and Her Times

article "The Long Road to Freedom" is published widely.

**1937**
Nellie's second anthology of newspaper columns, *More Leaves from Lantern Lane*, is published.

**1938**
Nellie McClung speaks at the Silver Jubilee celebration of the Women's Institute of Nova Scotia and then tours the province; she sails for Europe as the only woman in the Canadian delegation to the League of Nations in Geneva, Switzerland; first she attends ten days of talks at Interlaken with the controversial Oxford Group or MRA; she returns to Canada disillusioned with the League and enthusiastic about MRA despite its association by some with the Nazis.

**1940**
While attending a Board of Broadcast Governors meeting in Ottawa, Nellie McClung suffers a near-fatal heart attack; she resigns from the board and stops writing her weekly column "Leaves from Lantern Lane."

## Canada and the World

but he abdicates in order to marry Wallis Simpson.

**1937**
In Canada, Newton Rowell is appointed Co-chair of the Royal Commission on Dominion-Provincial Relations.

**1938**
Frank Buchman, founder of the Oxford Group, observes the nations of Europe preparing for war and conceives of a program to address the causes of war; his movement comes to be called Moral Re-Armament (MRA).

Hitler marches into Austria; Britain tries to appease Germany at Munich.

**1939**
The Second World War begins in September; Canada declares war on Germany and Italy.

**1940**
In Canada, women in Quebec are allowed to vote and run for office in provincial elections.

**McClung and Her Times**

**Canada and the World**

**1941**
Japan bombs Pearl Harbor on December 7; the U.S., Britain, and Canada declare war on Japan; intensive atomic research (the Manhattan Project) begins.

*As For Me and My House*, by Canadian Sinclair Ross, is published in New York.

Newton Rowell dies in Toronto after a long illness.

**1942**
The U.S. and Canada forcibly move Japanese citizens inland, away from the west coast of North America.

**1944**
In February, Jack McClung dies in Edmonton.

**1944**
The D-Day invasion by the Allies on June 6 begins the liberation of Europe from the Nazis.

**1945**
*The Stream Runs Fast*, the second volume of Nellie McClung's autobiography, is published; though depleted and heartsick she begins a new novel.

**1945**
Germany surrenders on May 8; the U.S. drops atomic bombs on Japan on August 6 and 9; Japan surrenders on September 2.

The United Nations (U.N.) Charter is signed on June 26 in San Francisco; Canada is one of the signatories.

**1946**
The McClungs celebrate their fiftieth wedding anniversary in August.

| McClung and Her Times | Canada and the World |
|---|---|

**CANADA AND THE WORLD**

**1948**
The U.N. adopts the Universal Declaration of Human Rights.

In Canada, Prince Edward Island finally repeals Prohibition; writer Frederick Philip Grove dies in Simcoe, Ontario.

**1950**
North Korea invades South Korea; U.N. forces land but are forced to withdraw.

**1951**
Nellie McClung dies in Victoria, B.C.; after her simple funeral she is buried at the Royal Oak Burial Park in Saanich, B.C.

**1951**
Charlotte Whitton is elected Canada's first female mayor in Ottawa.

**1954**
Agnes Macphail dies in Toronto.

**1958**
Ellen Fairclough becomes the first female cabinet minister in Canada.

# Acknowledgments

I would like to acknowledge a number of people who helped me with this book:

to the Provincial Archives of British Columbia, Alberta, and Manitoba; the National Archives of Canada; the Glenbow-Alberta Institute; and the City of Edmonton Archives, thank you for access to Nellie McClung's papers;

to Justice Margeurite Trussler and Justice Buzz McClung and his family, thank you for your blessings, both cautious and wise;

to Frances Wright, CEO and President of the Famous 5 Foundation, thank you for both valuable expertise and enthusiastic support;

to my dear friend Kathleen Redmond, my thanks for your boundless enthusiasm, your own memories, and your finely attuned ear;

to my noble editor Rhonda Bailey, thank you for careful editing and for taking a chance in the first place;

to Candace Savage, Marilyn Davis, and the late Mary Hallett, thank you for sharing your wonderful resource material;

to Nellie, who paved the way, wrote her own life, and from whom I have learned so much, thank you;

and finally, my profound gratitude and love go to Mark, Darian, Freya, and William Selander for allowing me time to write this story.

All the material in the book is gleaned from a careful examination of the life of Nellie Letitia Mooney McClung. For the most part, her words are her own. Occasionally, by way of illustration or clarity, I have placed those words in a fictitious historical context, which accurately mirrors Nellie's life and her true spirit. I take full responsibility for any inaccuracies be they large or small. My primary intent is to paint pictures that depict the life of a truly great Canadian.

# Sources Consulted

## Archival Records

Nellie McClung papers held in the British Columbia Archives as well as miscellaneous letters and clippings at the Glenbow-Alberta Institute, the Provincial Archives of Manitoba, the Provincial Archives of Alberta, the National Archives of Canada, and the City of Edmonton archives.

## Published Works

MCCLUNG, Nellie. *Clearing in the West: My Own Story*. Toronto: Thomas Allen 1935, reprint 1976.

MCCLUNG, Nellie. *The Stream Runs Fast: My Own Story*. Toronto: Thomas Allen, 1945.

MCCLUNG, Nellie. *The Next of Kin*. Toronto: Thomas Allen, 1917.

MCCLUNG, Nellie. *Sowing Seeds in Danny*. Toronto: William Briggs, 1908.

MCCLUNG, Nellie. *In Times Like These*. Toronto: McLeod and Allen, 1915.

HALLETT, Mary and Marilyn DAVIS. *Firing the Heather: The Life and Times of Nellie McClung*. Saskatoon: Fifth House Ltd., 1993.

SAVAGE, Candace, *Our Nell: A Scrapbook Biography of Nellie L. McClung*. Saskatoon: Western Producer Prairie Books, 1979.

CLEVERDON, Catherine. *The Women's Suffrage Movement in Canada. The Prairie Provinces*, Second edition. Toronto: University of Toronto Press, 1974.

ALLEN, Richard. *The Social Passion: Religion and Social Reform in Canada, 1914-1928*. Toronto: University of Toronto Press, 1971.

A variety of standard reference books on Canadian history including Grant McEwan's book *And Mighty Women too...* include a short biography of Nellie McClung.

# Index

DANGER

LE
PHOTOCOPILLAGE
TUE LE LIVRE

*Cet ouvrage
composé en New Caledonia
corps 12 sur 14
a été achevé d'imprimer
en mai deux mille trois
sur les presses de
Transcontinental Métrolitho
Sherbrooke (Québec).*